AF166133

PHYSICAL MAP OF
IRELAND

English Miles
0 5 10 20 30 40

Railways thus

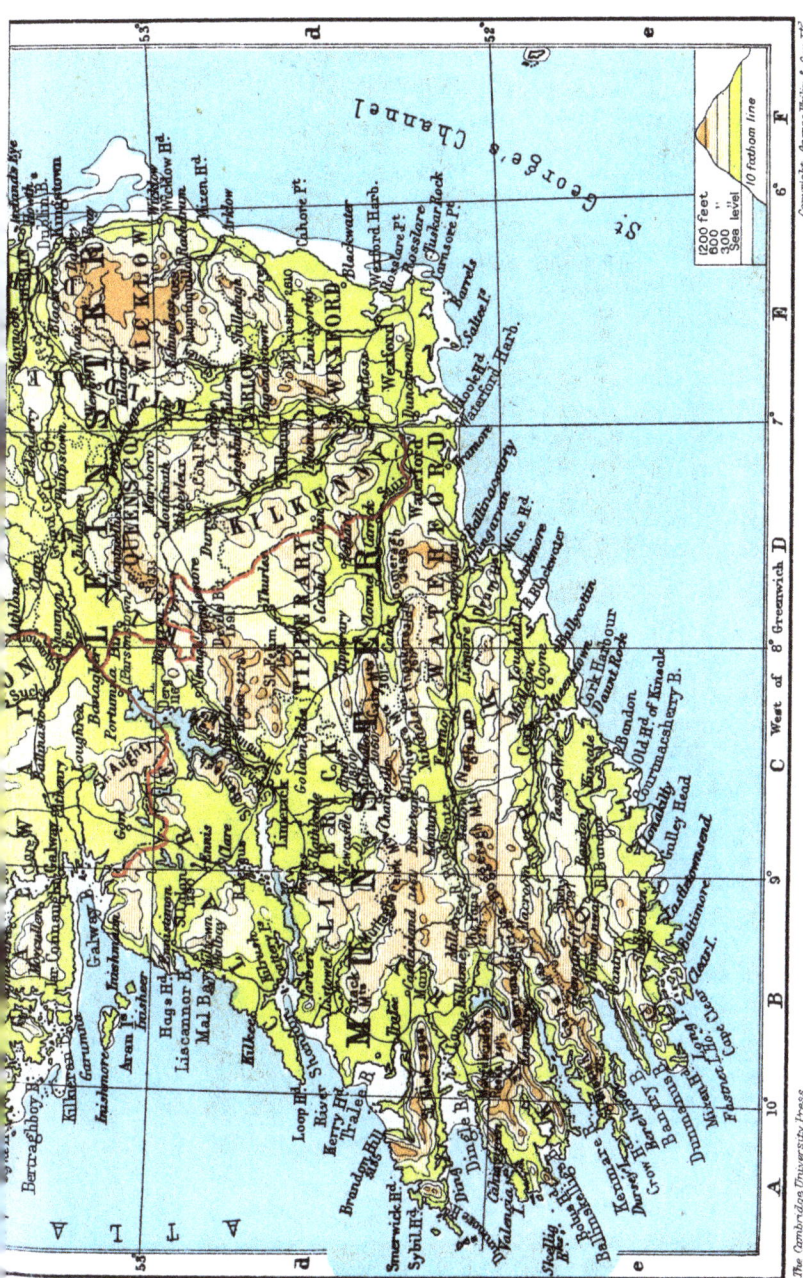

St. George's Channel

1200 feet
600 "
300 "
Sea level
10 fathom line

West of 8° Greenwich

The Cambridge University Press

THE PROVINCES OF IRELAND

Edited by
GEORGE FLETCHER, F.G.S., M.R.I.A.

IRELAND

IRELAND

Edited by

GEORGE FLETCHER, F.G.S., M.R.I.A.

With Maps, Diagrams and Illustrations

CAMBRIDGE

AT THE UNIVERSITY PRESS

1922

CAMBRIDGE
UNIVERSITY PRESS

University Printing House, Cambridge CB2 8BS, United Kingdom

Cambridge University Press is part of the University of Cambridge.

It furthers the University's mission by disseminating knowledge in the pursuit of
education, learning and research at the highest international levels of excellence.

www.cambridge.org
Information on this title: www.cambridge.org/9781316620021

First published 1922
First paperback edition 2016

A catalogue record for this publication is available from the British Library

ISBN 978-1-316-62002-1 Paperback

EDITOR'S NOTE

THE aim of this series is to offer, in a readable form, an account of the physical features of Ireland, and of the economic and social activities of its people. It deals therefore with matters of fact rather than with matters of opinion ; and, for this reason, it has happily been found possible to avoid political controversy. Ireland deserves to be known for her varied scenery, her wealth of archæological and antiquarian lore, her noble educational traditions, and her literary and artistic achievements. The progress and status of Ireland as an agricultural country are recognised and acknowledged, but her industrial potentialities have, until recently, been inadequately studied. The causes of the arrested development of her industries have been frequently dealt with. Her industrial resources, however, demand closer attention than they have hitherto received ; their economic significance has been enhanced by modern applications of scientific discovery and by world-wide economic changes. It is hoped that these pages may contribute to the growing movement in the direction of industrial reconstruction.

It is unusual to enlist the services of many writers in a work of modest dimensions, but it was felt that the more condensed an account, the more necessary was it to secure authoritative treatment. It is hoped that the names of the contributors will afford a sufficient guarantee that the desired end has been achieved. The editorial task of co-ordinating the work of these contributors has been made light and agreeable by their friendly co-operation.

The scope of the volumes and the mode of treatment adopted in them suggest their suitability for use in the higher forms of secondary schools. A notable reform is in course of accomplishment in the teaching of geography. The list of place-names is making room for the more rational study of a country in relation to those who dwell in it, and of these dwellers in relation to their environment.

In the planning of this series the need of a volume dealing with Ireland as a whole soon became manifest. Such matters as topography, geology, archæology, etc., have little to do with political boundaries, and it is not possible to present a true picture of Ireland in a volume dealing with a single province. On the other hand the detailed treatment appropriate to an account of a province would but blur the more comprehensive view which it is sought to give in this general sketch of Ireland as a whole.

This is a time of transition—" the old order changeth, yielding place to new,"—and the new order has not yet taken shape. The administrative system of the country will necessarily undergo profound modifications under the new *regime*. It is hoped that a brief account of the system as it existed until a few months ago will be of use and will assist an understanding of the nature of the changes brought about.

G. F.

August 1922

CONTENTS

CONTENTS

ILLUSTRATIONS

ILLUSTRATIONS xiii

IRELAND

MAPS AND DIAGRAMS

The illustrations on pp. 12, 15, 17, 21, 27, 28, 43, 44, 180, 188, 195, 215, 228, 229, 249 are reproduced from photographs by Messrs J. Valentine & Sons, Ltd. ; that on p. 165 from a photograph by Lord Walter Fitz-Gerald, by permission of the Kildare Archæological Society; that on p. 182 is reproduced by permission of the Galway Archæological and Historical Society; those on pp. 192, 208, 250 from photographs by Mr G. Fletcher ; that on p. 210 from a photograph by Mr W. D. Douglas ; that on p. 222 from a photograph by Messrs Brennan & Nixon ; that on p. 233 from a photograph by Mr Stuart, by permission of the White Star Line ; that on p. 241 from a photograph supplied by Messrs W. & R. Jacob & Co., Ltd. ; those on pp. 254, 272, 283 from photographs by Messrs Emery Walker, Ltd. ; those on pp. 257, 265, 270, 274 from photographs by Mr T. F. Geoghan ; that on p. 279 is reproduced by permission of Messrs Maclehose, Jackson & Co.

Acknowledgments are due to the Department of Agriculture and Technical Instruction for Ireland, and to the Royal Irish Academy for permission to use illustrations which have appeared in their publications.

IRELAND

TOPOGRAPHY

IF we carried out a series of soundings from the depths of the Atlantic towards its eastern edge we would find that the land which forms the Old World generally rises steeply from deep water. If we follow, for instance, the 100-fathom line—a line twice as far below the sea as the average surface of Ireland is above it—this line will be found to lie close to the coast along the whole shore of Africa, and also of south-western Europe. But off the coast of France this line bends far out to sea, and sweeping in a wide curve, again approaches the continental coast off southern Norway. In other words a great shelf exists here, covered with a mere film of water as compared with the ocean depths adjoining— an area which, though covered by sea, evidently belongs to the continent rather than to the ocean. On this platform the British Islands stand, and along with the North Sea occupy the greater part of it. Geological evidence shows that at least the higher portions of the shelf which are at present covered by water actually were dry land at a comparatively recent date. The British Isles must be looked on therefore as an integral portion of the continent of Europe, formerly continuous with it, though at present disconnected.

Ireland lies on the western portion of the shelf. The barrier of water (the Irish Sea) which separates it from

Great Britain is deeper than that which intervenes between the latter and the continental coast, and is without doubt older—that is, Ireland became a separate

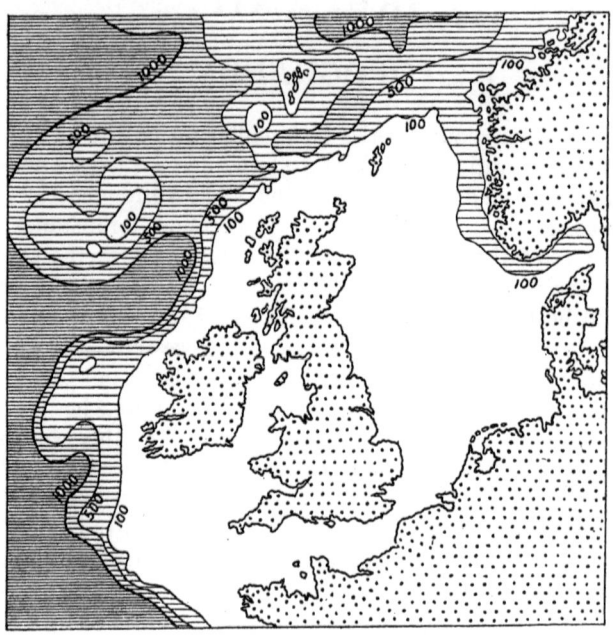

The Continental Shelf

island before Great Britain did.   The sea on the western side of Ireland is again rather deeper, and a hundred miles or so out from the coast we reach the edge of the shelf, and the bottom plunges down into oceanic depths.

As regards its position on the earth's surface, Ireland

lies between $51\frac{1}{2}°$ and $55\frac{1}{2}°$ north latitude—in the middle of the Temperate Zone—and between $5\frac{1}{2}°$ and $10\frac{1}{2}°$ west longitude. Roughly speaking it lies in the same latitude as Moscow, Kamtschatka, British Columbia and Labrador.

Ireland is much smaller than Great Britain, and it lies towards the west, where the sea, and the prevailing winds which blow in from the sea, are warmer; in consequence it is influenced to a greater degree than Great Britain by the conditions prevailing over the surrounding mass of water. Water being by its nature more slowly heated by the sun and more slowly cooled by radiation than land, it follows that the sea as compared with the land is cooler in summer and warmer in winter, and these conditions, imparted to the surrounding atmosphere, tend to produce higher winter temperatures and lower summer ones over Ireland than over Great Britain, and similarly, over the latter as compared with continental countries. These effects are particularly noticeable in the west of Ireland, where they obscure to a great extent the natural change of temperature which one expects to find between north and south. As a matter of fact, the isotherms, or lines of equal temperature, in the west of Ireland, both in summer and winter, run north and south instead of east and west, distance from the Atlantic counting for more than distance from the equator. In summer the warmest part of Ireland is in the south-east; in winter the coldest part is in the north-east. Much importance attaches to these facts, and the lesson which they teach should be borne in mind.

A comparison of the range of temperature found in Ireland and in England shows that while on the west coast of Ireland the difference between the average temperature of the coldest and warmest month is 16° F., the same comparison in the east of England gives no less than 24°. In comparison with the Continent the equability of the Irish climate is still more striking; thus, Kerry in January is as warm as Nice; in July it is as cool as Archangel.

The effect of the prevailing westerly winds, which in the main are responsible for these peculiarities of temperature, become very marked on the south and south - west coasts. The exposure here is extremely great, and often for miles inland hardly even a bush can raise its head. Many of even the larger islands have no tree more than a few feet in height.

As regards rainfall also, proximity to the western ocean is the leading factor; and the presence of mountains, usually the dominating condition, though still a potent influence, is nevertheless of secondary importance. The prevailing westerly winds, coming in off the Atlantic, are highly charged with moisture, and very heavy precipitation takes place among the hill-ranges of Kerry, Connemara and Donegal. The rainfall curves, as will be seen from the accompanying map, are largely parallel to the west coast, the main exception being in the south-east, where the highlands which rise from Waterford up to Wicklow deflect the 40-inch line in a wide curve almost up to Dublin. The driest areas in Ireland lie along the east coast, the minimum being reached in County Dublin.

Another effect of the presence of the warm ocean water around Ireland is the high degree of humidity or dampness of the air, and consequently of the soil. This has a direct and powerful influence on both animal and plant life ; it leads moreover to a prevalence of cloud, so that the amount of sunshine in Ireland is

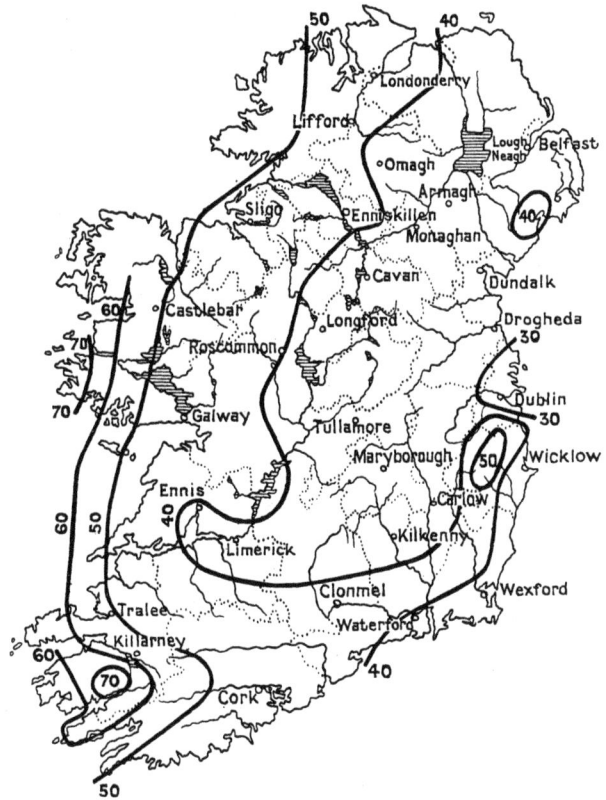

Irish Rainfall Map

reduced. The cloud in its turn by intercepting the sun's rays and by diminishing radiation tends to equalize the general temperature, and especially lessens the difference of temperature between day and night.

PHYSICAL FEATURES

Ireland is an irregular oval in shape, with the longer diameter running north-north-east and south-south-west. Its greatest length in a straight line, from Fair Head in Antrim to Mizen Head in Cork is 302 miles ; its greatest breadth, from Wicklow Head to Erris Head in Mayo, is 189 miles. Its area is 32,524 square miles. It is of compact form. No arms of the sea, large in proportion to the total size of the island, intervene between adjoining portions, as in the case of Greece or Denmark ; and the islands that lie off the coast are quite small as compared with the main mass of land.

Ireland is peculiar in having no back-bone parallel to its longer axis (*i.e.* N.N.E. and S.S.W.) with rivers flowing from it eastward and westward. Across the middle of the island, from east to west, a plain extends from sea to sea, with hilly country to the north and south of it. Yet the greater part of this plain is drained not by east and west streams, but by the Shannon, which, rising among the hills in the north, flows southward across the plain and cuts through the southern hills to the ocean. Several of the other main rivers have also courses that are likewise parallel to instead of at right angles to, the long axis of the country—that is, north or south instead of east and west. A consequence of this is that much of the water which falls on the country in the shape of rain reaches the sea by circuitous routes. Thus, the source of the Shannon, a river over 214 miles long, is distant only 23 miles from the sea at Sligo. The source of the Bann, 97 miles in length,

lies only 7 miles from the coast at Annalong and Carlingford Lough. The Barrow, 96 miles in length, has

Ireland
(*Land over 250 feet shown in black*)

tributaries which rise 24 miles from Dublin Bay. More
curious still, some of the streams, for instance, the

Barrow, which have their upper courses in the Central Plain, instead of flowing across the low ground to the sea,

Ireland
(*Land over 500 feet shown in black*)

flow *towards* the hills, and cut their way through them in deep narrow valleys.

The Irish mountains are mostly near the coast. Most of the highest hills—those of Wicklow, Carlow, Waterford, Cork, Kerry, Galway, Mayo, Sligo, Donegal, Derry, Antrim, and Down, rise within 25 miles of the sea. The counties with the largest percentage of low ground—Westmeath, Longford, Roscommon—lie in the centre of the country.

Lakes of all sizes are frequent, from large sheets of water like Lough Neagh (the largest lake in the British Isles) to the innumerable tiny lakelets of Connemara. They occur mainly in the north and west, and are almost absent from the south-east.

The coast is mostly irregular and much indented, especially in the north, west, and south, and is in many parts exceedingly bold.

We may now consider these physical features in rather more detail.

THE COAST

Taken as a whole, the coast of Ireland is much indented, with some tolerably large inlets and innumerable small bays, points and islets. From Dublin southward along the shores of Wicklow and Wexford great stretches of gravel-beach prevail. In Waterford the coast is higher, and often cliff-bound. The coast of Cork is full of pretty sheltered harbours lying inside bold promontories and islands. In West Cork and Kerry great sea-inlets, thirty miles in length, run far into the mountainous country. The Clare coast is inhospitable and devoid of harbours, mostly precipitous, the cliffs of Moher rising vertically to 668 ft. The Galway coast is low and exceedingly broken, with innumerable minor sinuosities and some large bays. The Mayo coast is similar, but with larger bays, peninsulas and islands, and some magnificent cliff scenery. In Sligo we have again a low much dissected coast-line. The Donegal shores resemble on the whole those of Galway, being mostly rather low and exceedingly broken ; but very bold scenery is found in the north and south. Most of the Derry coast is low and sandy, with high ground behind. The basaltic plateau of Antrim provides a very beautiful bold coast, with deep glens running in from the water. In Down, on the other hand, low reefs fringe the coast, running far out to sea, and very dangerous to shipping. The Louth coast is low and sandy ; that of Dublin is more diversified, with some bold headlands and islands.

The larger indentations of the coast may be grouped according to their origin. On the west coast mostly very old and hard rocks front the Atlantic, and to their presence there as an effectual breakwater is largely due the fact that Ireland exists at all. Wherever the more soluble and more easily denuded limestone forms the coast, the sea has penetrated for some distance —Donegal Bay, Sligo Bay, Killala Bay, Clew Bay, Galway Bay, Tralee Bay, and the great Kerry inlets have all low limestone at their heads or around their sides. The Aran Islands in Galway Bay are reefs of limestone corresponding to the rocks of North Clare, and point to the extent to which this rock has yielded to the forces of denudation. The inlets of Cork Harbour, Youghal Harbour, Waterford Harbour are sunken valleys cut by the Lee, Blackwater and Barrow when the land stood at a higher level than it does at present.

Belfast Lough represents the sunken valley of the Lagan, now greatly silted up at its head and the silts subsequently raised above sea-level, so that most of

Belfast is built on the old sea-bottom. Strangford Lough is simply a portion of the hummocky surface of Co. Down flooded by the sea, the tops of the hummocks still showing above the surface as numerous islands. The long narrow inlet of Killary Harbour and the broader Carlingford Lough are true fiords like those of Norway, with rocky bars at their mouths; they owe their present contours to glacial action.

No really large islands lie off the coast of Ireland—none so large as Lewis, Skye, Mull, Islay, Jura and Arran off the Scottish coast, nor even as Anglesey or the Isle of Wight. What islands there are are relatively small, and lie inshore, none of them being more than ten miles from the coast. The largest is the mountainous Achill Island in Mayo (50 square miles) separated by a very narrow strait. To the south of it Clare Island, Inishturk and Inishbofin are of some importance. The Aran Islands in Galway Bay are shelves of limestone clearly once connected with the limestone area of North Clare. Rathlin Island, off the Antrim coast, is a cliff-walled outlier of the basalt plateau of the north-east. Tory and North Aran lie off the Donegal coast. The islands off the south-west coast, such as the Blaskets and Skelligs, are often steep and lofty rock-masses, like mountain-crests rising from the waves. Others, such as Valencia Island and Dursey Island, are larger and less steep. The eastern coast is almost devoid of islands : the largest is Lambay off the Dublin coast, the monument of a very ancient volcano.

MOUNTAINS

The county of Donegal presents a series of ridges and valleys running north-east and south-west, the results of ancient folding of the earth's crust. The ridges seldom maintain a great average height, and the

Errigal (2466 ft.), Donegal Mountains

loftiest summits rise from them as isolated peaks—Errigal (2466 ft.), and Muckish (2197 ft.), far to the north-west, Slieve Snacht (2240 ft.), and Dooish (2147 ft.) on the next ridge to the southward ; the Croaghgorm or Bluestack range (2219 ft.) in the south of the county, and far to the north-east Slieve Snacht West (2019 ft.) on the peninsula of Inishowen.

The Tyrone and Derry Mountains lie east of the Donegal hills, from which they are separated by the ramifying valley of the Foyle. The high crest of the Sperrin Mountains, an ancient ridge of quartzite (Sawel, 2240 ft., Dart, 2040 ft.), dominates this region, the geology of which is very varied. To the north some basaltic hills rise which belong properly to the next group.

Eastward again, across the Bann valley, lava-flows have formed a high basaltic plateau which overhangs the east coast of Co. Antrim. This plateau had formerly a much greater extension, but the middle has collapsed to form the Bann valley. The highest points now remaining are Trostan (1817 ft.), and Slievenanee (1782 ft.).

The Mourne Mountains in the southern part of Co. Down form a bold compact granite group. Slieve Donard (the highest mountain in Ulster) rises to 2796 ft., and many peaks exceed 2000 ft.

Chiefly in Leitrim, but extending into the several counties round, several hill-groups rise, separated by valleys often containing considerable lakes. In the west, the bold limestone plateau of Ben Bulben looks down on the Atlantic. Around Lough Allen rise dark hills which yield coal and iron (Slieveanieran, 1922 ft.), and run north to the long high ridge of Cuilcagh (2188 ft.) on the borders of Cavan. The uplands extend northward as far as Lough Erne.

The Ox Mountains form a long high heathy ridge

(1778 ft.)—an ancient fold corresponding to those which formed the hills of Donegal—running south-west across western Sligo.

The western part of the counties of Mayo and Galway

Ben Bulben (1712 ft.)

are very wild and mountainous. These are separated into two groups by the wide inlet of Clew Bay and the depression which continues inland from it. On the northward side are the Nephinbeg range (2369 ft.), the isolated dome of Nephin (2646 ft.) and on Achill Island Slievemore (2204 ft.) and Croaghaun (2192 ft.), the latter descending sheer into the Atlantic in a great

cliff. South of Clew Bay rises the beautiful cone of
Croagh Patrick (2510 ft.), and around the fiord of

Slievemore (2204 ft.), Achill Island

Killary a number of high mountain groups of picturesque character are closely packed, with deep valleys

between—Mweelrea (2688) and its neighbours, the long ridge of Maam Turk (2307 ft.), the beautiful Twelve Bens (commonly called Twelve Pins) of Connemara (2395 ft.), and others. These groups are formed largely of quartzite.

From Dublin down to Waterford a great mass of granite extends, which fills almost the whole of Co. Wicklow with mountains, attaining in Lugnaquilla a height of 3039 ft., and having many points over 2000 ft. This range forms the largest continuous mass of high land in Ireland. The slates which formerly covered the granite, and have been worn off most of the summits, form picturesque hills along the flanks of the main mass. Mount Leinster (2610 ft.) and Blackstairs (2409 ft.) lying south of the Wicklow chain, are a continuation of the main fold.

Denudation of a very well-marked fold running down the centre of the southern half of Ireland has, by stripping off the former limestone covering, exposed the underlying slates and sandstones in a series of heathy hills extending from King's County south-west to Co. Limerick. In the north Slieve Bloom (1733 ft.) forms a long dark ridge; south of it the Devil's Bit and its neighbours are more diversified in shape; and beyond them a wider stretch of high ground culminates in Keeper Hill (2278 ft.). The Limestone Plain laps all round these hills, but southward the folds become more numerous, so that the ridges of slates and sandstones, running east and west, or north-east and south-west, dominate the whole country, and the limestone remains preserved only in the valleys between them.

The Galtees form a lofty and picturesque ridge (3015 ft.) southward of the Keeper range just mentioned, and the upland is continued westward at a lower eleva-

tion in the Ballyhoura Hills. South of them, between
the valleys of the Suir and Blackwater, the Knockmeal-
downs (2609 ft.) stand up in a series of steep cones ;
and a little east of them, the table-topped and cliff-
walled ridges of the Comeraghs (2597 ft.), embosoming

Macgillicuddy's Reeks (3414 ft.), Killarney

many romantic tarns, form a striking group. North
of the Comeraghs, across the valley of the Suir, Slievenaman rises solitary to a height of 2364 ft.

As one proceeds across Co. Cork into the extreme
south-west of Ireland, the country becomes more
and more mountainous, till the great promontories
which lie between Bantry Bay, Kenmare River, Dingle

B

Bay and Tralee Bay are filled with a tangle of high hills.
These highlands are almost continuous, and are separated
only by the deep sea-inlets just mentioned which cut
deep into them. In the south, a fine range, the Caha Mountains and Slieve Miskish, runs down the Berehaven promontory to its extremity. The broader promontory
lying between Kenmare River and Dingle Bay is likewise
most mountainous. At its landward end, near Killarney
rise the highest hills in Ireland, Macgillicuddy's Reeks
(3414 ft.). They form a noble group, with sharp conical
points, very steep slopes, and great precipices overlooking deep tarns. A high ridge runs from them south-
west to Derrynane, and another north-west to Drung
Hill (2104 ft.) overlooking Dingle Bay.

On the opposite side of Dingle Bay, occupying the
most northern of the Kerry promontories, another
high ridge rises quite detached at its landward end
from the main mass. At its eastern extremity Slieve
Mish (2796 ft.) rises over the town of Tralee, and far
to the westward the range terminates in the magnificent
ridge of Brandon (3127 ft.), which drops in huge cliffs
into the ocean. These Kerry hills are most picturesque,
and full of lakes and wild cliffs ; and the deep sea-inlets
that penetrate far into the land enhance the beauty of
their scenery.

THE CENTRAL PLAIN

If we draw a line east and west across Ireland from
Dublin Bay to Galway Bay, and another from Dundalk
Bay to Clew Bay and join them in the west by a line passing along the Galway chain of lakes, we enclose an area
of about 6000 square miles, more than half of which is less
than 250 ft. above sea-level, and of which only a number

of small patches in the north-east rise above 500 ft.
There is no hill in the whole area which reaches 1000 ft.

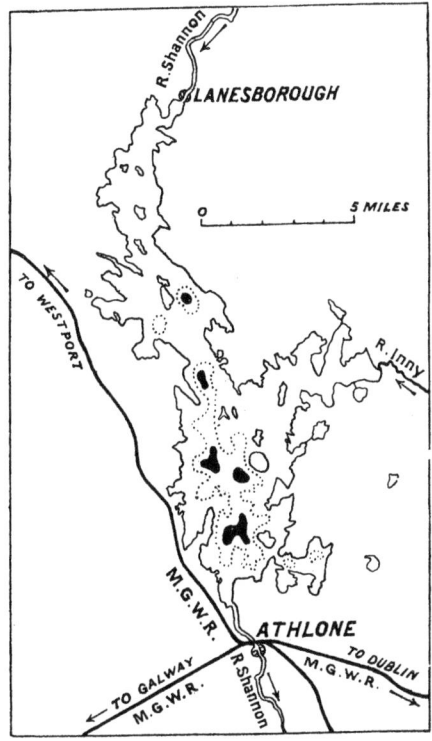

Lough Ree
(*Dotted line* = 5 *fathoms.   Black area* = *over* 10 *fathoms*)

The greater part of this plain is gently undulating ;
in the east it is quite diversified in parts, in the west
more featureless.   Save in the north-east, where Silurian
slates prevail, the plain is an almost unbroken sheet

of Carboniferous limestone, covered by Boulder-clay, esker-ridges, and peat bogs. The whole central portion is drained by the Shannon, which flows across the area from north to south, and by its tributaries. The Boyne drains the eastern part, and the western portion slopes to Galway Bay and Lough Corrib. The plain continues in places both north and south of the lines laid down above, filling wide areas between the hill-ranges which on both sides begin to break the surface, but its continuity soon ceases as one passes away from the central area.

No other portion of Ireland can vie with the Central Plain for continuity of low elevation. A considerable area of lowland surrounds Lough Neagh in the north-east; the eastern part of Co. Down is low and hummocky; and south-east Wexford is almost devoid of hills.

RIVERS

The peculiarity of the courses of many of the Irish rivers has already been mentioned (p. 6).

The Shannon is the largest river in the British Isles, and 214 miles in length. As its source, tradition points to a deep pool, the exit of an underground stream, on the western slope of Tiltinbane in Cavan, at an elevation of about 350 ft. Thence it foams down as a mountain stream and, dropping 186 ft. in 10 miles, enters Lough Allen, a pear-shaped lake 8 miles long, lying among high desolate hills. Flowing southward for a few miles, it receives from the west the drainage of Lough Gara and Lough Key, and assumes the ample breadth with many lake-like expansions and the slow progression which mark the greater part of its course. For 130 miles its fall is only 51 ft. At Lanesborough it expands

River Shannon, Athlone

into Lough Ree (p. 19), 18 miles long and 1 to 7 miles wide, with winding shores and numerous islands. Here it receives from the east the Inny, a considerable stream. Just beyond the lower end of this lake stands Athlone, an important centre, and as its name implies, the site of an ancient ford. Thence it winds through bogs and meadows, often with a complicated channel, for 40 miles to Portumna, receiving from the west the Suck, its largest tributary, and from the east the Brosna and Little Brosna. At Portumna, it enters the great expansion of Lough Derg, a winding lake 22 miles in length and mostly 1½ miles (at one point 9 miles) in breadth. So far its course has lain through the Limestone Plain, and since Lough Allen was left the only hills visible from it have been far on the horizon. Now, however, high ground closes in on both sides of the lake, till above Killaloe eminences of over 1500 ft. look down on it from either side. The Shannon flows through them in a narrow gorge, and having passed the barrier it bursts away in picturesque rapids, falling 97 ft. in 18 miles, and reaching sea-level at Limerick. Below that town its course is at first confined and muddy, but soon it widens out to several miles. A large flooded depression on the north side forms the island-studded estuary of the Fergus, draining central Clare. Thence, like an arm of the sea rather than a river,[1] it continues west, and, expanding to a width of nine miles, enters the Atlantic between the cliffs of Loop Head and those of Kerry Head. In its course the Shannon drains about one-sixth of the entire surface of Ireland. Its basin, except in the south and the extreme north, is very ill-defined, and a slight barrier in its course—a dam only about 160 ft. in height

[1] "The spacious Shenan spreading like a sea."—SPENSER.

—would turn its waters westward into Galway Bay,

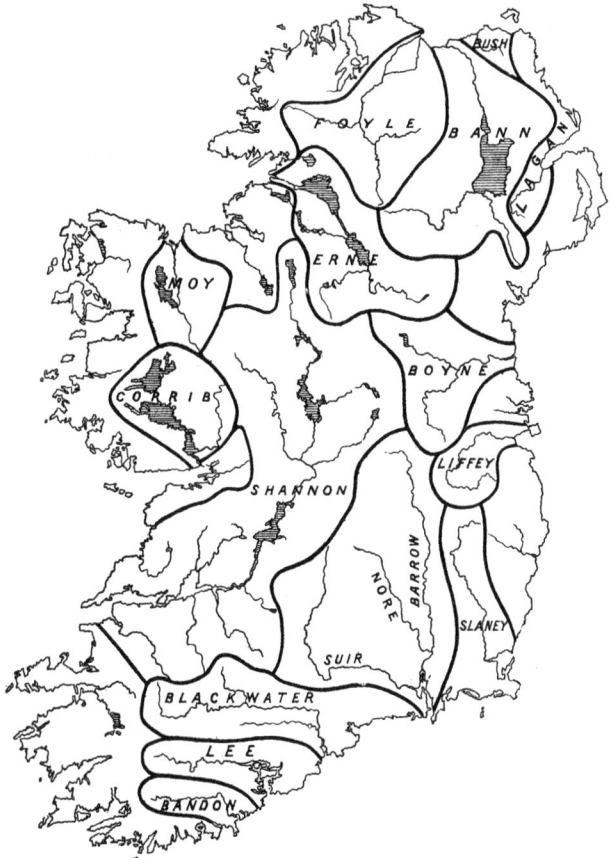

Irish River Basins

or eastward into the valley of the Boyne or Barrow.
How came it then to cut the deep gorge through the hills

at Killaloe, which, according to the present topography of the country form the line, not of least, but of greatest resistance ? It is clear that the present course of the river is a result of a long past topography, and the explanation is based on the different rate of decay of different kinds of rocks. There is evidence not only that the limestone has suffered greatly from denudation, and has now a much lower surface than it formerly possessed, but that thick beds of shales, etc., which once overlay it have also disappeared before the onslaught of rain and frost acting through countless centuries. Limestone is a soluble rock, and the Coal-measures which overlay it are formed of soft deposits. The Killaloe hills, on the other hand, are made of harder slates and sandstones. If we assume this high former level of the Central Plain we see that when the cutting of the Killaloe gorge began, the course of the river may well have been across the lowest ground available. As the Central Plain was slowly lowered, the river was able to keep pace with it by cutting down a narrow channel in the harder rocks. And so it has gone on to the present day. The cutting of the gorge still lags behind the lowering of the plain above it, as shown by the very slow flow of the river and the great dam of Lough Derg, held up by the want of depth in the gorge to drain it. Some day, perhaps, the river in the gorge will catch up, and by a quicker deepening of its bed drain the lake and produce a more rapid flow in its upper reaches.

The Barrow, Nore and Suir all rise on the long Slieve Bloom-Keeper fold that runs south-west down the south-central region of Ireland, and after somewhat divergent courses they unite to reach the sea in the broad estuary of Waterford Haven. All three display the peculiarity which has been explained at some length in dealing with the Shannon ; that is, while their upper courses lie across flat limestone areas, their lower courses are between hills. The explanation given in the case of the Shannon applies also to them. The three, which may be considered as a single river system, drain the greater part of south-eastern Ireland. The Barrow, rising on the north side of Slieve Bloom, flows for a short distance north and then west, after which it runs almost due south for about 70 miles to its mouth. Meandering through low-level marshes and bogs in its upper reaches it forms further down a very fine valley between high hills. The Nore, the central stream of the three, is smaller than the Barrow, and not, like it, generally navigable. The Suir, running far to the south, curves eastward and then takes a curious sudden bend to the north, and flows eastward with high hills on the southern bank, past Carrick-on-Suir and Waterford to join its companions.

The Blackwater, Lee and Bandon. The abrupt turn to the eastward of the Suir is the first indication as we go southward in Ireland of the profound influence which the east and west folding of the earth's crust in that region has had upon the course of the southern rivers. The Blackwater, Lee and Bandon Rivers, all rising at points much nearer to the sea than to their mouths, flow away to the east in parallel courses, and finally discharge by a sudden turn to the south. Their courses seem at first unaccountable, and may be best explained by a theory propounded by the late Prof. Jukes. The strong north-and-south crushing to which this area was subjected in very ancient times involved both the limestone and the underlying beds of slate and sandstone, throwing them into a series of east-and-west waves. Subsequent denudation left a tolerably flat surface sloping towards the south, across which the drainage flowed. Owing to the folding, this surface was formed of parallel beds of limestone and of slate. By the more rapid removal of the soluble limestone, east-and-west valleys were deepened by tributary streams more rapidly than the main north-and-south valleys. In consequence, the drainage got more and more diverted from the old main channels, till by the continued excavation of the limestone troughs they now carry the main drainage, save where near their mouths the rate of cutting down of the original north-and-south channels has been sufficiently rapid to keep them open. Remains of the old north-and-south channels can still be traced in many places across the slate ridges that divide the limestone valleys down which the rivers now flow.

The Blackwater, rising on the borders of Kerry, flows southward for some miles till it is captured by the head of a very long east-and-west limestone trough which it follows for 55 miles to Cappoquin ; there it suddenly turns south, and cutting through great ribs of slate in a gorge about 400 ft. deep, reaches the sea at Youghal. The Lee has a somewhat similar course, but its mouth is more complicated, having a double turn to the southward, and being flooded by the sea over its low limestone troughs.

The Slaney, rising on the west side of the Wicklow mountains, runs southward, and, cutting across a low part of the great granite axis of Leinster, becomes tidal at Enniscorthy and enters the broad, shallow Wexford Harbour at the ancient port of the same name.

Enniscorthy

The **Ovoca River,** famous for its scenery, drains most of the eastern slopes of the Wicklow highlands, and reaches the sea at Arklow.

The **Liffey,** rising near the north end of the Leinster chain, runs first west, then north, and finally east, to enter the sea at Dublin.

The **Boyne** is a much larger river than any of the three

River Bann at Coleraine

preceding. It has a wide-branching system of tributaries coming mostly from the north-west, the main stream having a north-easterly course from its source on Carbury Hill in Kildare. From Navan on, it often forms a gorge in the limestone through which it flows ; it becomes tidal near Drogheda, to which port, 4 miles from its narrow mouth, fairly large steamers have access.

The **Lagan** is a small river flowing from Slieve Croob across Co. Down to enter the sea at Belfast.

The Bann and Foyle between them drain the greater part of Northern Ulster. The former rises (as the Upper Bann), on the Mourne Mountains and flows north into Lough Neagh ; as the Lower Bann it leaves the opposite end of the lake and flows north to meet the sea below Coleraine. It drains the whole Lough Neagh basin, in which several considerable streams find their way to that lake, the largest being the Blackwater in the south-west, and the Main in the north. The depression in which the lake lies, and through which its drainage reaches the northern ocean, is due to a collapse of the central part of the basaltic plateau which still stands high both to the east and to the west.

The Foyle drains a hilly area lying in Tyrone and Donegal by means of numerous considerable tributaries from east and west. The main stream, broad and tidal in its lower part, flows north-east to enter Lough Foyle below Londonderry.

The Erne is a remarkable river, flowing north-west through a broad, low limestone trough, over much of which it spreads as a system of mazy lakes full of low promontories, bays and islands. Lough Gowna (where it rises), Lough Oughter, and Upper Lough Erne are of this complex pattern ; Lower Lough Erne is larger, and in its lower part more open. At the end of the last-mentioned lake the river descends in foaming cascades through a narrow gorge, and reaches the sea in Donegal Bay below Ballyshannon.

The rough mountainous mass in West Mayo and West Galway diverts to the north and to the south the drainage of the great plain which lies behind. The Moy, flowing northward to enter the sea below Ballina at the head of Killala Bay, drains the northern part of this area and also Lough Conn. Southward, the string of large lakes which lie behind Connemara—Loughs Carra, Mask, and Corrib—drains southward from one to another ; below Lough Corrib a short sudden drop through the city of Galway brings this drainage into Galway Bay (as the River Corrib). The Claregalway River, entering Lough Corrib, carries the drainage of a large area of the plain to the eastward.

LAKES

Ireland is essentially a land of lakes. Over 1050 square miles are covered by fresh water ; this amounts to about one-thirtieth of the entire area of the country. Reckoned by *number*, lakes are most abundant in the mountainous districts of the west coast, from Kerry to Donegal ; but with regard to size, the largest lakes lie in the low grounds further inland. Many of the more important lakes have been referred to already when the rivers of Ireland were being dealt with, and they may be now passed by in rapid review.

Lough Neagh is the largest sheet of fresh water in the British Isles ; it is roughly rectangular in shape and has an area of 153 square miles. Its formation is due, as stated on p. 29, to a sinking of portion of the basaltic plateau which occupies the north-east of Ireland. From its sandy and stony margins, the bottom drops rather rapidly to a remarkably uniform depth of 40 to 50 ft., so that the lake-bed itself forms a plain, which is interrupted only by a group of reefs in the centre, and a little valley down the middle of the arm which runs towards the exit channel in the north-west, and where at one point the bottom sinks to a depth of 102 ft.

below the surface. The lake now occupies the middle portion of a wide depression, over much of which it spread in ancient times; its present surface is only a little over 40 ft. above mean sea-level.

The Shannon Lakes.—The several large lakes (Loughs Allen, Ree, Derg) which form part of the course of the Shannon have been referred to in the description of the course of that river (p. 20).

The Erne Lakes.—The remarkable island-filled lakes which to a great extent form the course of the River Erne are mentioned similarly where that river is dealt with (p. 29).

The Corrib-Conn Chain of Lakes.—Where the western margin of the Central Plain meets the edge of the great mountain mass of old rocks which forms West Mayo and West Galway a string of large lakes has been formed along the north-and-south junction. In the north is Lough Conn, with its continuation Lough Cullin, 12 miles long by about 3 miles broad, with the great quartzite dome of Nephin (2646 ft.) towering over it on the west. It drains northward from its southern end by the River Moy into Killala Bay. Going south we cross a low watershed and reach the winding Lough Carra, a lake of wonderfully clear green water fed by springs, which empties southward into the adjoining Lough Mask, 10 miles long by about 4 miles wide, and 191 ft. in depth, with the high bare ridge of the Partry mountains impending on its western side. It drains by an underground passage through the limestone into Lough Corrib, 32 miles in length from the head of its long north-western arm to its southern extremity. Lough Corrib is very irregular in shape and in depth, and full of points, reefs and islands. The northern

part is much the deepest (152 ft.). From near its
southern end the River Corrib issues as a broad, slow

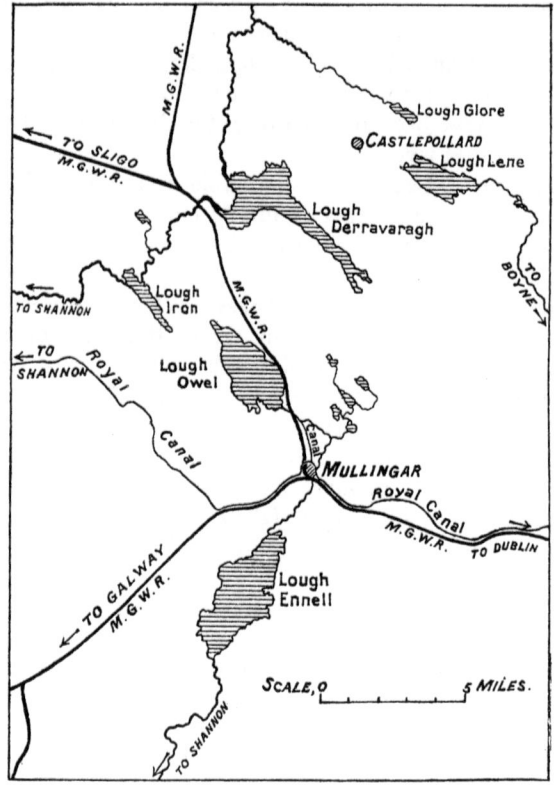

The Westmeath Lakes

stream, which at Galway plunges suddenly down to
the sea.

Groups of lakes much smaller in size, though still

noteworthy, lie in Westmeath, in south Cavan, Sligo, etc. The Lakes of Killarney, famous for their beauty, are of no considerable dimensions.

TRAFFIC ROUTES

The immediate problem of Irish railway construction, when railway transport began to supersede road and canal traffic before the middle of the nineteenth century, was the joining up of Dublin, the capital of the country, with Belfast and Londonderry in the north, Galway in the west, and Cork and Limerick in the south-west, and the inclusion *en route* of as many as possible of the more important towns and villages. But none of the main lines which now link these towns was constructed at one time as a single enterprise.

The Great Northern Railway.—As regards the northern route, a line was built early along the coast from Dublin to Drogheda, where the deep gorge of the Boyne offered a serious obstacle and caused a pause in construction. At the other end, the nucleus of the old " Ulster Railway " was formed by the building of a line south - westward up the valley of the Lagan from Belfast through Lisburn, Lurgan and Portadown to Armagh, a course which presented no engineering difficulties. Subsequently the " Belfast and Dublin Junction Railway " linked the two systems by joining Portadown and Drogheda. The Boyne was crossed by what still remains the largest bridge in Ireland, the rails being some 200 ft. above the river below. A second serious obstacle was the mountain barrier on the frontiers of Leinster and Ulster, about Slieve Gullion. This was crossed by climbing, without tunnelling, the line rising from sea-level at Dundalk to

C

over 400 ft. between that town and Goraghwood ; near the latter place it crosses the gorge of the Bessbrook

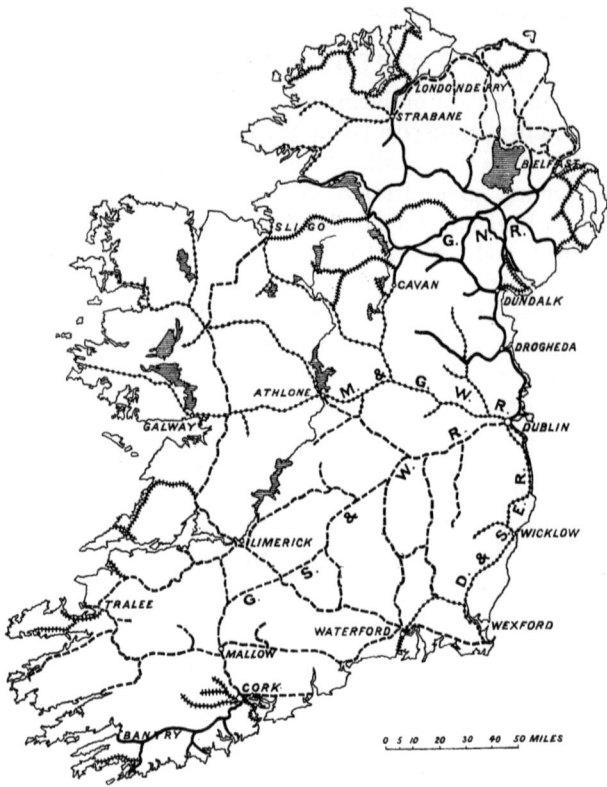

Irish Railway Systems

River on a lofty masonry viaduct of many arches. The extension of the line northward from Portadown to Londonderry through the county of Tyrone offered no difficulties other than some stiff climbing. With many branch lines afterwards constructed, including an important route north-westward from Dundalk through Clones and Enniskillen to Omagh (and on to Londonderry) and to the Atlantic at Bundoran, this whole system became the Great Northern Railway (Ireland), with a total mileage of 533 miles. Although the greater part of the system runs through hilly country, river-valleys were so availed of that (save those mentioned above) no great bridges were required, nor any long tunnel, except where the branch from Goraghwood to Armagh pierces the ridge above the former place.

The Midland Great Western Railway.—The route to Galway from Dublin lies across the Central Plain from sea to sea. No obstacle intervenes, and it would have been possible to cross the country without ever rising to 300 ft. above sea-level. But the necessity of serving the principal towns *en route*—Mullingar, Athlone and Ballinasloe—led to a selection of a route north of the direct line, and of a rise to over 400 ft. about the first - mentioned place. The Dublin - Mullingar section of the line follows closely the edge of the pre-existing Royal Canal—a plan tending to reduce cost of construction, but, on account of the numerous curves which resulted, introducing difficulties in these days of high speeds. The main line from Dublin to Galway is, like the country, rather featureless, and the iron bridge across the Shannon at Athlone is a welcome change from the alternation of low embankments and cuttings. From Mullingar a branch which is longer than the main line runs north-west, skirts the upper waters of the Shannon for some miles, and reaches the important port of Sligo. From Athlone an important branch—also longer than the main line—runs north-westward over the grass country of Roscommon and Mayo to meet the Atlantic at Clew Bay and Killala Bay, but the seaports which it serves there are unimportant. An extension constructed some twenty years ago carries the main line on from Galway right across Connemara to the Atlantic at Clifden.

With several branches which need not be particularly mentioned, the total mileage of the system is 539 ; the nature of the country through which it runs—very largely grassland with few towns—causes the traffic on the line to be less than on the Great Northern.

The Great Southern and Western Railway. — The country which lies between Dublin and Cork is studded with bold groups of hills, some of them of imposing height (the Galtees rise to over 3000 ft.). Between the hill-groups the valleys are often wide and flat, the remnants of the old limestone plain which was destroyed by the ancient crushing and up-thrusting of the crust into mountains. Once the flank of the Wicklow mountains was turned some 10 miles west of Dublin, the road was open to Maryborough, whence a broad trough was available for railway construction running south-west between Slieve Bloom, the Devil's Bit, and the Keeper range on the north and the Kilkenny uplands and Galtees on the south. Mallow was reached by a swing to the southward, but here, on the other side of the fertile valley of the Blackwater, a high ridge runs east and west, barring the way to the south. The main road takes advantage of a gap directly south of Mallow (no doubt this gap, which must have been an important thoroughfare long before the days of roads, determined the position of the town), and the railway follows the same route, climbing out of Mallow to a height of nearly 500 ft., whence it drops in 13 miles to sea-level at Cork. This southern slope necessitates the steepest climb on any Irish main line, the gradient being for a time 1 in 60, and even in these days of powerful locomotives often requiring the employment of a second engine.

By the building of branches and the absorption of other lines the system now serves the greater part of the south and south-west of Ireland ; it is interesting from the geographic standpoint to note the advantage which it was possible to take of the river-systems of the district. Thus the north-and-south valleys of the Barrow and Nore, which the main line crosses near their heads in Queen's County, permitted of the easy construction of branches running far southward, one of them eventually reaching Wexford, the other Waterford. The east-and-west valleys which form so noticeable a feature of the south of Ireland allowed easy access from Mallow westward to Killarney, and eastward to Dungarvan and thence to Waterford ; similarly from Cork to Youghal and Macroom, and from Clonmel to Waterford.

Comparatively recently the Great Southern and Western Railway took over the lines of the Waterford, Limerick and Western Railway, and thus acquired an important route extending from Waterford through Limerick, Ennis, Athenry (where it crosses the main line to Galway), and Claremorris (where the Mayo line is crossed), to Sligo. The whole Great Southern and Western system thus formed is the largest railway system in Ireland, amounting to 1083 miles.

The lines of the other Irish railways are shorter than the three described above, and as they are each confined to one of the provinces, they are dealt with in the other volumes of the series, where certain local features of the railway system are also considered.

Canals.—The later years of the eighteenth century saw considerable activity in canal building in Ireland, and there was then every prospect that this mode of conveyance would have a long and successful vogue. But the nineteenth century was still young, and many of the canals had had less than forty years of life, when the era of railroads arrived. This new and more rapid means of conveyance was a serious blow to the canals, reducing traffic on most of them and jeopardising the prospects of some ; at the present time one or two of the waterways are derelict.

Two canals in Ireland of great importance are unusual in being quite independent of rivers or river-valleys. They run from Dublin westward across the Central Plain to the Shannon. The more southern one, the GRAND CANAL, starting from the Dublin docks, forms the southern boundary of Dublin city, and, crossing the River Liffey near Naas, where the stream bends southward, runs almost due west through Tullamore to the Shannon near Banagher, whence it is continued to Ballinasloe. It attains its highest level (279 ft. above the sea and 164 ft. above the Shannon) at a point 26 miles from Dublin, where it is fed by large springs coming from under the Curragh of Kildare, a few miles to the southward. Several branches connect the main canal with towns on either hand.

The ROYAL CANAL starts from the north side of Dublin harbour, and, skirting the city, formed, until the inclusion of the northern townships, its boundary on

that side. It runs a little to the north of westward to
Mullingar, where it attains its highest point (324 ft.
over sea-level), and is fed from Lough Owel, a lake of
wonderfully clear water produced by springs. Thence
it passes by Ballymahon, and, turning to the northward,
enters the Shannon at Cloondara west of Longford.

The Shannon must have been an important traffic
route even in prehistoric times. Its long and placid
course from Lough Allen to Lough Derg—a distance of
some 130 miles, with a fall of only 50 ft.—was no doubt
a frequented highway in the days of dug-out canoes ;
and in modern days the whole of this stretch has been
rendered navigable for tolerably large boats by the
provision of weirs and locks where the depth of water
was insufficient owing to a slope in the river bottom.

At Killaloe, at the southern end of Lough Derg, the
river abruptly changes its character. It drops suddenly,
rushing over ledges of rock, and falls 97 ft. in 18 miles.
At Limerick it reaches sea-level, and widens into a great
estuary. By means of several stretches of canal, a
waterway has been constructed along this difficult
portion of the river's course, so that boats can proceed
from the Atlantic to the upper end of Lough Allen, a
distance of about 200 miles.

The remaining canals of Ireland are referred to in
the volumes devoted to the Irish Provinces, but the
following waterways may be enumerated :—

The Barrow Navigation, which utilises that river from
its mouth, is continued northward as a canal from Athy
to join the main line of the Grand Canal at Robertstown
in Kildare ; the Ballinamore and Ballyconnell Canal,
which joins the head-waters of the Shannon with those
of the Erne, whence the Ulster Canal continues the

waterway through Clones and Monaghan and down the River Blackwater to Lough Neagh : Lough Neagh is in turn connected with the River Lagan and Belfast by the Lagan Canal, running eastward ; with the northern sea by the Lower Bann Navigation, which follows the course of that river ; and with Newry and Carlingford Lough by the Newry Canal, which in the northern part of its course utilises the Upper Bann from Lough Neagh to a point above Portadown. The Boyne Navigation, designed to permit of water traffic from Drogheda to Navan, is now in a state of disrepair.

Roads.—Before the days of constructed roads, traffic from town to town, conducted on foot or on horseback, took the "line of least resistance," avoiding the higher hills on the one hand, and on the other hand low-lying tracts which were marshy or liable to inundation. The hills are there still, but much of the low country has been drained, and new roads now traverse it, with the old roads often traceable on the higher lands adjoining. The increase of heavy traffic also rendered unsuitable many hill-roads, and longer routes with easier grades were constructed. The course of the old lines of traffic often determined the position of a town, as at an important ford or pass a village would frequently arise or a fortress be built for purposes of defence ; conversely, the towns determined in many cases the course of the roads, as communication had to be provided from one town to the next. In the more difficult parts of the country the course of the roads, which often at first sight appears haphazard, is mostly the result of deliberate choice, based on experience extending back through centuries. Hence, for instance, when railways came to be constructed and science to be applied to the question of routes, it often proved that the engineer's level only confirmed the choice of route already indicated by the ancient road.

As regards the Irish roads in general, not much need be said here. The finest roads are those in mountain districts, where modern skill has been brought to bear, and where steady gradients replace the breakneck course of the old bridle-paths. In such districts, too, the rocks are generally hard and the road-surfaces in consequence good. Throughout the Central Plain, where drainage is often bad and no better rock than limestone available, the surface is frequently bad, and after rain sometimes atrocious. The experienced traveller in these areas will use by-roads as far as possible if he desires comfort. The result of recent measures of local government, combined with the more frequent use of the steam roller, has been greatly to improve the roads in many parts of Ireland. Motor traffic, while causing a demand for better surfaces, is in itself very destructive of such surfaces, and by rendering the roads less safe and less pleasant, tends to diminish other kinds of traffic, especially cycling and walking.

COUNTIES AND TOWNS

Ireland, 32,524 square miles in total area, with a population (in 1911) of 4,390,219, is for administrative purposes divided into four Provinces—Ulster, Leinster, Connaught and Munster—and into 32 counties. The Provinces are of approximately equal size, and form a tolerably natural division of the country into north, east, west and south. The counties are much more variable in size. The smallest is Louth (316 square miles), the largest, Cork (2890 square miles). Just as in the United States we find the smallest states in the east, where the country is longest settled and the population most dense, while in the west much larger tracts have been subsequently included as units, so in Ireland the smaller counties lie in the long-settled and more fertile east, the larger counties in the more recently reclaimed and more mountainous west. The counties are in their turn divided into baronies, baronies into parishes, and parishes into townlands. In the towns the ultimate division is into wards and parishes.

The dividing up of the country has followed no definite scheme, and the boundaries comparatively seldom follow the leading natural features. It has been carried out through many centuries, and local history and tradition, and conditions prevailing at the time, have chiefly influenced it.

The counties are distributed among the Provinces as under :—

ULSTER—Donegal, Londonderry, Tyrone, Antrim, Down, Armagh, Monaghan, Fermanagh, Cavan.

LEINSTER—Louth, Meath, Westmeath, Longford, Dublin, Kildare, King's County, Queen's County, Wicklow, Carlow, Kilkenny, Wexford.

CONNAUGHT — Leitrim, Sligo, Mayo, Roscommon, Galway.

MUNSTER—Clare, Tipperary, Limerick, Waterford, Cork, Kerry.

The most important towns in Ireland—Dublin (population 304,802), Belfast (386,947) and Cork (76,673) —are situated on the seaboard in the eastern half, between the most northern and most southern points

of the coast. Here also are situated Londonderry
(40,780), Coleraine (7785), Newry (11,963), Dundalk
(13,128), Drogheda (12,501), Wexford (11,531) and
Waterford (27,464). The western coast, though better
provided with harbours, has not nearly so many important towns upon it—Sligo (11,163), Galway (13,255),

City Hall, Belfast

Limerick (38,518), Tralee (10,300). Inland, towns of
considerable size are few—Enniskillen (4847), Athlone
(7472) and Kilkenny (10,514) being among the more
important.

All the larger coastal towns are intimately associated
as regards their positions with harbours and river-
mouths, and it is clear that their sites were originally
determined by convenience of access to the sea on the

Waterford, from the West

one hand, and often, on the other hand, access to the interior by means of a waterway ; their positions had also reference in most cases to the lowest point at which the river could be forded and a thoroughfare along the coast maintained. Sometimes questions of defence played a leading part as regards selection of site, as in the case of Cork and Limerick, which were built each on an island ; Enniskillen is an example of an inland town similarly placed. Athlone marks the site of a highly important ford across the great barrier of the Shannon.

The presence of a larger number of important towns on the east coast than on the west coast is due mainly to the fact that the lands in the east are richer than those in the west, and consequently have supported a larger population. The fact that the eastern ports are the natural points of arrival and departure of traffic to and from England and Scotland has also exercised an important influence.

THE IRISH PROVINCES

FROM time immemorial Ireland was divided into five provinces, so that the expression " the five-fifths of Ireland " was constantly used poetically to describe the whole island. These provinces, as Professor John MacNeill has lately shown, were Ulster, Connaught, Munster, and two Leinsters—North and South— though in most books two Munsters replace the two Leinsters. The boundaries of these were all supposed to meet at the hill of Usnagh in Westmeath, where, according to Joyce, the great stone forming the meeting-point is still to be seen. It is obvious that no possible division of Munster could make the two portions reach so far. There seems the same difficulty as regards Leinster; yet it is possible that the dividing line ran from the headwaters of the Slaney north-westward by those of the Boyne, and so to Usnagh.

A new fifth province is found in historic times, viz. Meath. This is said to have been formed in the second century of our era by cutting off a portion from each of the older provinces in order to form a domain for the supreme king of the whole island.

Ulster.—At the period of the Anglo-Norman invasion the old kingdom of Ulster had long ceased to exist. In its stead were three independent kingdoms—Uladh proper, or Ulidia, the shrunken remnant of the old kingdom east of the Bann, Lough Neagh, and the Newry River; Oirghialla, comprising the modern Fermanagh, Monaghan, Armagh, and part of Louth; and the king-dom of the Northern Ui Niaill, the modern Donegal, Derry, and Tyrone.

Thus the old province did not include Cavan, but did include the part of Louth north of the Dee. The English invasion shattered the two kingdoms of Uladh and Oirghialla. The whole province was granted to John de Courcy—if he could conquer it—"*si a force la peust conquerre*," says the French poet. He over-ran the sea coast from Downpatrick to Coleraine, and from his conquests were formed five bailiwicks, or counties, as they are sometimes called.[1] He also

[1] Orpen: "Earldom of Ulster," *Jour. R. Soc. of Antiquaries.* References. Vol. xliii., p. 133.

seems to have held Carlingford and the northern peninsula of Louth.

The rest of Louth seems to have been overrun from Meath, and to have been treated by King John as not included in De Courcy's grant. Hence English Uriell, as it was called, became detached from Ulster, and was ultimately included in Leinster.[1]

The invasion of Edward Bruce shattered the English settlements in the rest of the province. A few baronies along the coast of Down and Antrim remained in the hands of the settlers; the rest of the modern counties of Antrim and Down were recovered by the Irish— the greater part being seized by a branch of the O'Neills. The main stock of the O'Neills extended their power over the rest of Ulster, with the exception of Tirconnell, the country of the O'Donnells. Outside the old limits of the province they brought the O'Reillys of East Breffni under their influence; hence this district — the modern County Cavan — became detached from Connaught, and was ultimately included in Ulster.[2]

When, in the sixteenth century, an attempt was made to divide Ulster into counties, the actual divisions between the clans were taken into account. The counties of Down and Antrim had persisted in name at least, and the division between them seems to have been made to coincide with the actual limits between the lands of two branches of the O'Neills of Clandeboy.

To Down were allocated, besides the lands in

[1] Orpen : *Ireland under the Normans.*
[2] Cavan is said to have been detached from Connaught to reduce the size of that province. It was at one time intended to add it to Leinster.

English hands and part of Clandeboy, the territories held by the MacGennisses and the MacCartans.

Armagh took in the O'Hanlons of Orior, the O'Neills of the Fews, the lands of the See of Armagh, as much of the lands of the O'Neills of Tyrone as lay south and east of the River Blackwater, and the MacCanns.

Monaghan represents the district ruled over by MacMahon, Cavan that by O'Reilly, Fermanagh that by MacGuire. Derry is made up of the lands of the O'Cahanes and the north-eastern portion of Tirowen proper. The rest of the O'Neill territories form the County of Tyrone.

Finally, the O'Donnell territory of Tirconnell was formed into the County of Donegal, and to this was added O'Dougherty's land of Inishowen, for long a subject of dispute between the O'Neills and O'Donnells.[1]

Leinster and Meath.—Leinster in the sixteenth century comprised the former provinces of Leinster and Meath. It did not include the territory of Ely O'Carroll (the present baronies of Clonlish and Ballybrit in King's County); otherwise it corresponded to the present province, except that County Longford seems sometimes to have been looked on as part of Connaught.

The old kingdom of Meath had disappeared utterly. Its former ruling family, the O'Melaghlins, still possessed a small district in Westmeath, the modern baronies of Clonlonan and Brawney, in the south-west of the county. Such Irish clans as survived in the rest of the former kingdom had no political connection one with another. They were the O'Ferralls, whose territory of Annaly

---

[1] Inquisitions between 1606 and 1610 defined the boundaries in Ulster and Connaught. Falkiner, *Illustrations of Irish History and Topography.*

forms the modern County Longford, the MacGeoghegans of Moycashel, the Foxes of Kilcoursey, the O'Molloys of Fercal (the modern Eglish, Ballyboy and Ballycowan) and the MacCoghlans of Delvin, the modern Garrycastle. (These last districts are in King's County.) The O'Maddens of Siol Anmchada in Co. Galway held the parish of Lusmagh in the modern King's County.

The old kingdom of Leinster still survived, but within greatly shrunken limits. The last to call himself King of Leinster was Cahir MacInnycrosse MacMurrough Kavanagh, who began to rule in 1530. Carlow and North Wexford were the chief seats of the MacMurrough power. The O'Byrnes and O'Tooles of Wicklow were more loosely under their control. The O'Mores of Leix and O'Conors of Offaly do not appear in any way subject to them. The MacGillapatricks, descendants of the former rulers of the sub-kingdom of Ossory, still held the district known as Upper Ossory, the modern baronies of Upper Woods, Clandonagh and Clarmallagh in Queen's County.

The English Lands.—These fall into two groups. First, there was the thoroughly settled district of the valleys of the Liffey and the Boyne. All of the modern counties of Meath, Kildare, and Louth, and almost all Dublin, were held by families of Norman or English descent. These counties are constantly alluded to as the four obedient shires. Most of the modern Westmeath comes under the same definition, being then included in Meath.

The Pale.—Within this district lay " the Pale," strictly speaking the lands lying inside the fortified line running from the sea at Dundalk inland by Ardee to Trim, and then by Navan, Clane, and Naas to the Liffey at Kilcullen. From there it went by Ballymore Eustace

D

along the foot of the mountains by Rathmore, Rath-
coole, Tallaght to the sea at Dalkey.

Outside this line the great feudal families, Nugents,
Dillons and others, especially the earls of Kildare, were
practically supreme, each in their own district.

The south of Wexford, comprising the modern
baronies of Forth, Bargy, Shelmalier, and Shelburn,
had also been thoroughly colonised. Here there was no
one great family, but many small proprietors. For all
practical purposes this portion of Wexford might be
considered as part of the Pale. Most of the modern
County Kilkenny had also been thoroughly colonised,
and the city of Kilkenny, with several smaller fortified
towns were centres of English influence. The power
of the earls of Ormond was predominant over the
whole county.

Modern Counties and Old Divisions

Meath.—Annaly had, in part at least, been overrun
by the first invaders; but the O'Ferralls had expelled
the settlers during the course of the fourteenth century.
On their submission to the Crown in the sixteenth century
their lands were formed into the County of Longford.
Westmeath was split off from Meath in or about 1542.
To it were assigned the lands of the O'Melaghlins
and MacGeoghegans. The remaining Irish districts of
Meath, viz. Fercal, Delvin MacCoghlan, and Fox's
country were allotted to the newly-formed King's
County.

Leinster.—Of the remaining counties of the modern
province, Kilkenny represents the old kingdom of
Ossory, less the portion retained by the MacGillapatricks—Upper Ossory—which now forms three

baronies in Queen's County. Ossory fell to the share of one of the five Marshall co-heiresses in 1247.

Dublin is made up of the old Danish kingdom, the possessions of the archbishop and other ecclesiastical proprietors in Dublin, and the lands of some Irish clans. Originally it included the mountainous districts to the south which were the property of the sees of Dublin and Glendalough, and the coast district as far as Arklow, the direct lordship over which was reserved by the Crown from the lands confirmed to Strongbow by Henry II.

Kildare, Carlow, and Wexford appear to have originated from the division of the Lordship of Leinster between the five sisters and co-heiresses of Walter Marshall in 1247.[1]

They were formed by grouping various Irish territories, and hence do not correspond exactly to any of the old sub-kingdoms. Carlow appears originally to have extended to the sea at Arklow, taking in parts of South Wicklow and North Wexford. A large part of this district was never subdued, and in the fourteenth century the Irish recovered almost the whole of the modern County Carlow, together with North Wexford and the whole of the modern Wicklow.

Finally, the hill country held by the O'Tooles and O'Byrnes was formed into a separate county in 1606 ; the district more directly under the MacMurroughs was divided, that to the east of Mount Leinster falling

[1] Carlow with Old Ross passed to the Dukes of Norfolk ; Wexford to the De Valences, and then to various other families. These lordships were confiscated by Henry VIII by the Act of Absentees. It does not appear certain when the modern boundaries of Carlow and Wexford were fixed.

to Wexford, that to the west remaining as County Carlow. Thus the small size of the modern counties of Dublin and Carlow is accounted for on historical grounds, which partly depend on physical features, since the Normans effected no permanent conquests in the hill districts, and the Irish who had taken refuge therein recovered a great part of the adjacent lowlands in the fourteenth century. King's County and Queen's County first took shape under Philip and Mary in 1556. The Leinster part of King's County represents on the whole that part of the old district of Offaly which the English grantees failed to subdue—that portion which they had subdued being now in Kildare. The remainder of the County is made up of the Meath districts of Fercal, Delvin MacCoghlan, and Fox's country of Kilcoursey, and of the Munster district of Ely O'Carrol. The inhabitants of this last district had maintained their freedom against the attacks of the earls of Ormond ; and, on their submission to the Crown in the sixteenth century, petitioned and obtained that they should not be included in Tipperary, the county of their hereditary enemies.

Queen's County was made up from the territories of Upper Ossory, Leix, and part of Offaly, namely, the barony of Tinnahinch held by O'Dunne, and Portnahinch, portion of the lands of O'Dempsey.

Leix, together with some scattered lands, had been the share of the fifth of the Marshall co-heiresses, but had been completely recovered by the Irish during the fourteenth century.

Finally, the County of Louth, representing the portion of Oirghialla which had been permanently conquered and occupied, came to be considered as part of Leinster.

As indicated under the heading of Ulster, the southern portion was settled from Leinster and Meath ; and King John apparently did not look on it as included in the grant to De Courcy.

Munster.—The modern province approximates closely to the ancient limits, although the district of Ely O'Carroll has been transferred to Leinster, and a small portion of the former Thomond to Connaught.

Five of the present counties—those east and south of the Shannon — have existed at least from the thirteenth century, and are amongst those the creation of which is popularly—though without any sufficient evidence—ascribed to King John. Of these, Waterford corresponds to as much of the old territory of the Deisi as lay between the Suir and the sea. The other four were formed to some extent by grouping various Irish districts ; but it is impossible to say on what principle this grouping was carried out, or when the division was made. The boundaries of Cork, Limerick, Kerry, and Tipperary do not appear in any way to correspond to the actual political divisions of Munster at the time of the Anglo-Norman invasion. The grants of Henry II and John speak of the kingdoms of Cork and Limerick, but tell us nothing as to the exact boundaries between them ; and it seems doubtful to which—if, indeed, to either—we are to assign North Kerry, West Limerick, and East and South Tipperary. The greater part of these five counties was soon overrun by the invaders, but the Irish held their ground in the mountains of South Kerry and West Cork, and in the broken country to the south-east of Lough Derg. All attempts to conquer Thomond west of the Shannon failed ; and in the fourteenth century the Irish recovered the greater part of Thomond east of the Shannon, *i.e.* North Tipperary and portions of Limerick. During the same period they recovered South Kerry as far as the River Maine, and West Cork, as far, roughly, as the line Kinsale, Cork, Mallow, and Charleville.

In the sixteenth century we hear of a new county—Desmond—*i.e.* the portions of Cork and Kerry more directly under the rule of the family of MacCarthy Mor. This district took in the four southern baronies of the modern Kerry, together with those of Bere and Bantry in Cork, and apparently the Barony of Duhallow, now in the latter county. In 1606 this county was abolished, and divided, very unevenly, between its neighbours.

Tipperary was granted as a " Liberty " or " County Palatine " to the first earl of Ormond in 1328. The church lands, as usual, were excepted from this grant, and formed a special county under the name of Cross Tipperary. To this latter was added the Irish district of Ara in 1606. The County Palatine was resumed by James I, but revived at the Restoration. In the new grant the former territories of Cross Tipperary were included, hence the two counties were amalgamated into one. The separate Palatinate jurisdiction was finally abolished on the attainder of the second duke of Ormond in 1715. The O'Carrolls of Ely had maintained their independence against the earls of Ormond, and in the sixteenth century succeeded in inducing the government to include their lands in the newly-formed King's County, rather than in Tipperary, the county of their hereditary enemies.

Co. Clare represents the ancient Thomond west of the Shannon. King Murrough O'Brien submitted to

Henry VIII in 1542 and was created earl of Thomond. When Thomond west of the Shannon was reduced to shireground in 1576, the name Clare was given to it, from a castle, Clar-atha-da-choradh (the ford of the two weirs), situated close to Ennis, which for a short time was made the administrative centre. Geographical reasons led Sir Henry Sidney about 1579 to transfer the county to Connaught ; but the influence of the earls of Thomond was strong enough to have this arrangement set aside, and to rejoin the county to the province to which it had belonged since the race of Cormac Cas had wrested it from Connaught and made " sword land " of it in the fourth century. In more recent times two parishes in the extreme north-east angle, bordering on Lough Derg, have been transferred to Co. Galway.

Connaught.—Connaught in the time of St Patrick comprised the whole country west of the Shannon, together with Leitrim, part of Cavan and, possibly, part of Longford. The eastern part of Co. Cavan was annexed at a later period. What is now the county Clare was conquered at an early period by the Munster men ; and has since, except for a short time during the sixteenth century, been included in that province. The modern Leitrim and Cavan formed in the twelfth century the sub-kingdom of Breffni, the " rough third of Connacht " as the annalists call it. Its king, Tiernan O'Rourke, had made himself master of Meath also, with the curious result that Henry II's grant of Meath to de Lacy was interpreted as including Breffni. No permanent settlement of this district was made by the invaders, though grants were given and some temporary conquests made. The greater part of the remainder of the province was,

after a complicated series of grants and regrants, given
to the De Burgo or Burke family by King Henry III
the king reserving certain territories near the Shannon.
These he either left to the Irish or divided among lesser
grantees. Hence arose two counties—Roscommon, those
portions not in the De Burgo grant, and Connaught,
the remainder of the province (excluding Breffni).
After the murder of earl William de Burgo in 1333,
some of his kinsmen seized on his Connaught possessions,
and threw off all dependence on the Crown. The Irish
recovered a great portion of the province, including all
the districts reserved from the de Burgo grant.

When in the sixteenth century English power once
more made itself felt beyond the Shannon, the present
counties were formed. In their formation existing
political divisions were followed. Hence O'Rourke's
lordship of West Breffni became the Co. Leitrim, as
O'Reilly's land of East Breffni was turned into
Co. Cavan. Sligo was formed of the lands held by
O'Conor Sligo and his dependent chiefs, Mayo from
those ruled over by the " Lower MacWilliam "—one
of the Hibernicised de Burgo chiefs.

In dividing the remainder of the province between
the counties of Galway and Roscommon, neither the
older bounds of the latter county, nor existing political
divisions seem to have been strictly followed. The
River Suck was taken to be the boundary for a great
part of its course, thus assigning some of the lands
of the O'Kellys to Galway, and some to Roscommon.
The lands of O'Conor Roe, O'Conor Don, MacDermott
and their dependents, with a small district belonging
to one of the Burkes, made up the rest of this latter
county.

The kingdom of Connaught persisted, in name at least, until 1384, although greatly weakened by the feuds of the various branches of the royal house of O'Conor, and overshadowed by the power of the de Burgo earls.

In 1385, a year after the death of Ruaidhri O'Conor, the claims of two rivals for the crown, Turlough Don, son of Aedh, and Turlough Roe, son of Felim, were met by a division of the territory which was directly subject to the O'Conors. Hence arose the two houses of O'Conor Don of Ballintubber and O'Conor Roe of Roscommon. It was probably intended to divide between the two competitors the rents and services due from the other Irish clans in Breffni, Sligo, and Ui Maine, and we find for some years the phrase, " Half King of Connaught," used of the rival O'Conors. But, as a matter of fact, the O'Conors were too weak to impose their supremacy on their neighbours ; and at the opening of the sixteenth century each of the great clans, O'Reilly, O'Rourke, O'Kelly, and O'Madden appears as quite independent ; while a branch of the O'Conors seated at Sligo had brought under their rule the clans in what is now the County of Sligo, and were quite free from the parent house. Of the lesser clans along the western seaboard, the O'Malleys were dependent on the Lower, and the O'Shaughnessys and O'Heynes on the Upper MacWilliam.

Much detailed information with regard to the origin of the modern Irish counties will be found in an article, " The Counties of Ireland, their Origin, Constitution and Gradual Development," in C. Litton Falkiner's book *Illustrations of Irish History*. For the earlier period, especially for the division of the lordship of

Leinster among the five daughters and co-heiresses of William Marshall, earl of Pembroke, on the death of his son Walter, see Orpen, *The Normans in Ireland*.

THE GENERAL GEOLOGY OF IRELAND

THE geological history and structure of Ireland are closely bound up with those of north-western Europe. Certain events have occurred at certain epochs, separated in time by many millions of years, which have left results that remain conspicuous in the landscapes of the present day. As is well known, the divisions of past time are marked out by the successive prevalence on the earth of certain types of life; the rocks containing a particular group of animal types are known as a geological " system," while the time occupied in their formation is styled a " period." For every system there is thus a period bearing the same name. The names have been somewhat arbitrarily chosen, and are explained in geological text-books.

In north-western Europe the earliest known systems are represented by the remains of a worn-down continental surface formed of crystalline rocks—micaschists, quartzites, and granular marbles, which are the highly altered forms of clays, sandstones, and ordinary limestones. These are penetrated by numerous rocks that were once molten, which have mostly consolidated as granite; and much of the alteration of the ancient systems is due to the invasion of these masses from hot cauldrons down below. The intimate penetration of granite into pre-existing schistose rocks has given rise to extensive tracts of banded gneiss.

The first well marked group of life-forms on the globe is found in the CAMBRIAN system. All that goes before may be styled PRE-CAMBRIAN or ARCHÆAN. The Cambrian beds are succeeded by the ORDOVICIAN (or LOWER SILURIAN) and SILURIAN (or UPPER SILURIAN) systems. At the close of the latter period a great wrinkling of the earth's crust took place in our area, folding up the sea-floor from south-east to north-west, and extending the borders of the Pre-Cambrian continent. These folds, which are conspicuous in Scotland, are styled *Caledonian*. On this new land-surface the DEVONIAN strata were laid down, mostly representing dry regions, where the rocks decayed under changes of temperature and wind-action, while their detritus was washed into the plains and hollows by occasional storms. Lakes also received the pebbly and sandy waste from the hills, and the typical deposits of this period are known as the "Old Red Sandstone." To the south of the Irish area, however, the Devonian sea laid down muds, which are now hardened into slates. Then the CARBONIFEROUS period opened, among the first beds being limestones, which represent the remains of a multitude of shell-fish and corals that lived in a broad extension of the sea. Later, a gradual upheaval provided swampy flats, on which great forests of old-world plants spread luxuriantly, yielding in time beds of coal interstratified with shales and sandstones. A second wrinkling of the crust followed, and the Carboniferous and Devonian strata, and much of the older materials, became folded from south to north ; a series of ridges, styled *Armorican* from the region of Brittany, thus runs across the

Irish area from east to west.   The PERMIAN and TRIASSIC
periods that followed are consequently marked for the
most part by terrestrial beds, and desert conditions
once more prevailed in Triassic times.   The JURASSIC
and CRETACEOUS periods saw an extension of the sea
from the south-east into parts of the Irish area.   This
area, however, still lay on the margin of a continent
stretching towards Greenland.   Then, at the opening of
the great time-division known as the CAINOZOIC or
TERTIARY era, serious disturbances of the crust allowed
lavas to flow out in the north-east of Ireland, deluging
large districts of Cretaceous rocks that were now raised
above the sea.   The EOCENE and OLIGOCENE periods
are represented by these volcanic masses, and the
whole Irish area seems to have remained dry land
through the succeeding MIOCENE and PLIOCENE periods.
The Atlantic Ocean spread northward during these
latter periods, while modern Europe was growing out of
an eastern sea.   Ireland, broken from its former land-
connexions on the west, became joined on to the new
continent, of which it now forms the western outpost.
Recent subsidences in the HUMAN or QUATERNARY
era have converted it into an island, separated from
Great Britain by merely shallow seas.   In this era
it came, with the world at large, under the influence
of the " Glacial epoch," when a general refrigera-
tion allowed snow and ice to cover practically all the
country.

   This long series of events is recorded in the present
surface-features and the rocks of Ireland.   Relics of
the PRE-CAMBRIAN continent appear in the north and
west.   These have been remoulded by the Caledonian
folding, and their main structural lines run in conse-

quence north-east and south-west. The crystalline rocks of the Ox Mountains and of central Donegal illustrate the permeation of mica-schists and other highly altered strata by floods of granite from below. The mica-schists and the occasional grey marbles yield fertile soils, but are frequently reared into mountainous ridges which receive a heavy rainfall. The quartzites, on account of their hardness, weather out in conspicuous crags and domes, of which the group of the Twelve Bens and the Maam Turc Mountains in Connemara are fine examples. Errigal and Muckish in Co. Donegal rise with grey rocky crests above rounded moors of mica-schist. Rugged features are also furnished by long bars of intrusive dolerite, following the general Caledonian trend; these dark masses are especially conspicuous in Inishowen.

The noblest cliffs in the British Isles, those of Slieve League in Donegal and Minaun in Achill Island, are formed of Pre-Cambrian quartzite. The wild and desolate west of Mayo is carved for the most part out of mica-schist and quartzite, and the quartzite dome of Nephin above Lough Conn rivals the Twelve Bens of Connemara.

A moorland rarely traversed by strangers, lying between Omagh and Cookstown in the county of Tyrone, reveals a core of gneisses and schists, and another exposure occurs in the extreme north-east of Co. Antrim. Similar rocks no doubt underlie a large part of the country.

CAMBRIAN strata are known only in the eastern area, from Dublin Bay to near Wicklow, and from Cahore Pt. to the coast south-west of Wexford. They have yielded the problematic but typical fossil *Oldhamia* and a few traces of worms. The hard slates form broken country, and the associated quartzites give rise to bare knobs dominating the landscape, like Ben Edar on Howth, the beautiful cone of the Great Sugarloaf in Co. Wicklow,

Cambrian Country of Co. Wicklow, from the sea

and the weirdly castellated range of the Mountains of Forth in Co. Wexford.

ORDOVICIAN and (UPPER) SILURIAN strata are associated conformably in Ireland, and consist of slates, shales, and sandstones, with only a few beds of limestone. In the west of the Dingle Promontory and along the flanks of the Leinster Chain volcanic rocks

occur among them ; but these nowhere produce the
striking scenery that arises from their presence in North
Wales. Hummocky country prevails in a broad tri-
angular Ordovician and Silurian area that extends from
near Longford to the coast of Co. Down. Granite rises
from Newry to Slieve Croob along the axis of this
region, which is continued into Scotland as the Southern
Uplands. Away west, on both sides of Killary Harbour,
Ordovician conglomerates and barren sandstones, passing upward into Silurian strata, form mountainous
masses, such as Mweelrea and Formnamore, while the
grand quartzite cone of Croagh Patrick on the south
side of Clew Bay has proved to be of Silurian age. The
beds here rest unconformably on the Pre-Cambrian
series, the lowest Ordovician (*Arenig*) strata being
known in the Killary district.

Throughout central and southern Ireland cores of
Ordovician and Silurian slates and sandstones, which
are mostly of *Llandovery* age, appear in the Armorican
upfolds, surrounded by scarped hills of Old Red Sandstone. The latter series unconformably overlies the
strata that were uptilted and contorted by the Caledonian folding, so that in the Curlew Hills near Boyle,
in the Slieve Bloom and Devil's Bit ranges, and in the
Galtee Mountains, we find both the epochs of earth-
crumpling admirably recorded. The section on the
north bank of the Suir at Waterford thus shows on a
bold scale inclined Old Red Sandstone conglomerates
overlying vertical and folded Ordovician slates.

The Leinster Chain, however, owes its supremacy
to the Caledonian folding. In the core of the great
complex arch of Ordovician strata, which runs from Dun
Laoghaire to the Waterford coast, the largest exposure

of granite in the British Isles now forms an almost
continuous moorland. The high though rounded domes
of this early Devonian igneous mass are nobly con-
trasted with the more dissected scenery of the foothills.

Valley of Consequent Stream
(*E. flank of the Leinster chain, Glenmalure, Co. Wicklow*)

Where the streams pass from the granite to the
Ordovician slates, waterfalls and gorge - cutting are
frequent features.

The OLD RED SANDSTONE, which was formed from
the waste of the Caledonian ranges, appears in a broad
area stretching from Enniskillen almost to Cookstown.

It is usually conglomeratic, and represents the most resisting of the materials that were worn from the pre-existing highlands.   It weathers out in consequence in

Cirque-head in Old Red Sandstone Conglomerate, Coumshingaun, Comeragh Mts., Co. Waterford

scarped and barren masses, from which the more yielding Carboniferous strata have been removed by denudation. The Armorican ranges in southern Ireland are thus largely formed by Old Red Sandstone, the overlying Carboniferous Slate or Limestone remaining only in the

E

synclinal or downfolded bands. In the Dingle Promontory, a series of sandstones and conglomerates of doubtful age, but older than the true Old Red Sandstone, which overlies them unconformably, is known as the *Dingle Beds*, and provides an interesting problem in stratigraphy.

The CARBONIFEROUS sea at first deposited muddy beds in the extreme south, which now appear as slates ; but generally the extensive growth of shell-bearing organisms has given rise to a vast series of limestones, with some shaly deposits, formed around islands, where the old Caledonian land-surface still rose above the sea. The beds become sandy in the north and north-west, showing nearness to a shore-line, and at Ballycastle in Co. Antrim there is an interesting coalfield of Lower Carboniferous age. The central plain of Ireland, stretching from the Galtee Mountains and Slievenaman to Donegal Bay, and from Dublin to Galway and the Ox Mountains, owes its uniformity to the broad covering of Carboniferous Limestone, which allowed it to be worn down to a peneplain, firstly at the close of the Armorican movements, and then far later, after the Cretaceous sea had left the country. The beds of sandstone, shale, and coal, mostly of Upper Carboniferous age, that at one time overlay the limestone, have left only a few outlying relics, such as the Lough Allen, Tyrone and Leinster Coalfields. Near Coal Island in Tyrone the coal-bearing beds pass eastward beneath Triassic strata ; but the denudation that evidently took place before this post-Carboniferous cover was laid down implies that no vast area of concealed coal can be expected, unless other fields, preserved in synclinals, can be traced under the basalt to the east.

The Leinster coalfield consists of a high outlier between Maryborough and Kilkenny. South-west of it, on Slieve Ardagh in Tipperary, coal is also worked. The Coal-Measure areas that form somewhat bleak country in Clare, Limerick, and northern Kerry are unproductive.

PERMIAN beds are known only as small patches of magnesian limestone at Holywood on Belfast Lough and near Stewartstown, and as a conglomerate of blocks of Carboniferous Limestone at Armagh. The TRIASSIC sandstones and marls do not occur south of an outlier near Kingscourt in Co. Cavan; but they evidently covered at one time much more of the post-Armorican peneplain. They form red soils around Belfast, where they have been protected by the Cainozoic lavas, and they are traceable west of Lough Neagh and in the east of Co. Londonderry. The covering of lava similarly preserves patches of LOWER JURASSIC strata in north-eastern Ireland; but it is probable that the sea retreated towards the English area before Middle Jurassic times. The famous oolitic limestones of the Cotswolds and Portland are consequently not found in Ireland. The CRETACEOUS system is similarly limited, consisting of greensands passing up into glauconitic chalk, and a hard chalk, the "white limestone" of Co. Antrim. The whole series is about 100 ft. in thickness, and probably had a considerable extension southward. Cretaceous flints and chalk occur on the sea-floor off the west coast of Ireland, and large flints are suggestively washed up on the south coast of Wexford.

The "white limestone" appears as a conspicuous band, quarried for lime, under the grim black basaltic lavas of the plateaus of Antrim and Londonderry.

These Cainozoic lavas include, in the fine cliffs of Bengore, the columnar basaltic flow that forms the famous Giant's Causeway. The granite of the Mourne Mountains, and the slightly older gabbro mass of

Basalt on Chalk, Cave Hill, nr. Belfast, Co. Antrim

Carlingford Mountain, doubtless represent subterranean cauldrons from which some of the lavas reached the surface. The Mourne Mountains, with their immature and broken outlines, are thus a comparatively recent addition to the geological structure of Ireland.

Little is known of the history of the Irish area after early Cainozoic times. A general slope of the country probably determined at this date the southward course of the Shannon, the Suck, the Slaney, the Barrow, and

Weathering of Cainozoic Granite, Mourne Mountains

the Nore. Denudation carved away the Cainozoic lavas, leaving the scarped edges of the present plateaus; the post-Armorican peneplain that had become uplifted was attacked, until the limestone was reduced to its present low level across the plain and in the river-valleys of the south. In the GLACIAL epoch, ice-flows from Scotland invaded the north as far as Londonderry and Antrim towns, and pressed up from the Irish Sea to a height of 1500 ft. against the east flank of the Leinster Chain. Glaciers that were generated in a great snow-dome about the region of Lower Lough Erne and along Slieve Bawn spread over the plain and far to southward and to westward, and conflicted on the east with the Irish Channel ice from Scotland. A warmer epoch followed, after which local centres of precipitation, such as the Donegal and Connemara hills and the Leinster Chain, sent out newly extended glaciers over much of the country that had previously been covered by a more continental type of ice-sheet. The *boulder-clays* that were deposited from the two types of glaciers, consisting of the material picked up from the deeply weathered surface of the country and carried forward by the ice, have profoundly influenced the present surface. Where they were irregularly distributed in the ice, these boulder-clays, as they finally melted out, formed the rounded hog-backed hills known as *drumlins*.

The sub-glacial drainage, when ice occupied all the lowlands, is still marked by lines of gravel hills, or *eskers*, which are casts of the channels by which the water escaped from the stagnating ice-sheets. "Dry gaps," like the ravine known as the Scalp, near Dublin, mark, in many parts of the country, the overflow-channels of lost glacial lakes.

The discovery of a pre-Glacial shore-line near the present one in southern Ireland shows that the late Cainozoic sea penetrated the river-valleys of the south. The west coast similarly indicates submergence, and such inlets as Bantry Bay and Killary Harbour are due to the drop of the whole country towards the Atlantic.

The broad downfold now occupied by the Irish Channel
also admitted the sea before Glacial times, since marine
shells are found freely mixed with the deposits of the

Ravine of the Scalp, near Dublin
*(From its south-western edge, the channel of overflow of a
glacial lake)*

epoch of maximum glaciation on the eastern coast.
As the ice melted and the land rose, a dry passage no
doubt was established, across which the Irish mammals
of the present day entered the country. The occurrence
of submerged peat and forest beds round the whole of

Ireland points to a still more recent subsidence, whereby the insular nature of the region was finally determined. A slight uplift has brought some of these post-Glacial forest beds, covered by blue marine muds, once more near to the present sea-level, and *raised beaches*, such as that which forms the Curran of Larne, have arisen since neolithic man was in the country. The rivers in general have been able to cut notches in the margin of the Glacial peneplain, and the Liffey falls at Leixlip and the rapids of the Shannon at Castleconnell alike attest the latest upward movement of the Irish region.

Ireland is not very rich in mineral ores, though *copper ore* was at one time largely extracted in the south. The only *iron ores* at present worked are those associated with the decay of basalt in Eocene or Oligocene times in the north-eastern area. These deposits represent a pause in the series of eruptions, during which tropical climatic conditions allowed of a breaking-up of the silicates and a concentration of aluminium and iron hydroxide. The iron ores are in consequence often aluminous, and true *bauxites* occur, which are worked at present for the alum trade rather than for aluminium.

The Irish *coal-seams* are bituminous north of a line between Dublin and Galway, and are anthracitic south of this, as in the Leinster coalfield. It is believed that a number of good seams still await working in the partly concealed coalfield of Tyrone.

The grey Carboniferous limestone is commonly used as a building-stone, and the Lower Carboniferous sandstones of the north-west have similarly proved effective. Black marbles occur in the Carboniferous series at Galway City and Kilkenny, and red varieties in the south of Co. Cork. The unique green marble of Conne-

Karst Landscape, under windy conditions. Carboniferous Limestone, the Burren, Co. Clare

mara is an altered Pre-Cambrian limestone marked by bands and knots of Serpentine.

The soils of Ireland are commonly good loams, and are rarely deficient in lime, owing to the diffusion of pebbles of limestone in the glacial drifts. But the Old Red Sandstone and the quartzite mountain lands are naturally barren, except where covered by glacial material. In upraised wind-swept areas the Carboniferous Limestone may be practically devoid of soil, and karst conditions may prevail. Peat occupies large areas of the central plain, and furnishes a cheap fuel to the inhabitants. Experiments are being made in the development of forests on boglands that have been cut away.

POPULATION—LANGUAGE— RELIGION

THE NATIVE TRADITIONS

THE native Irish traditions of the peopling of the country are enshrined in certain ancient tracts on history, preserved in various manuscripts. The most important of these is *Leabhar Gabhála* or the " Book of Invasions." According to these legends, Ireland has been peopled by a succession of immigrations, the modern Celtic-speaking population being the last of the series. Such traditions, though doubtless much mixed with fable, are worth attention. The universal tendency of ancient peoples is to represent themselves as *autochthonous*, that is, as belonging essentially to the soil on which they are found. When we observe them deriving their descent from elsewhere, the probability is that a true tradition is enshrined in their belief.

According to the native historians, the first immigration was a small party of three men and fifty women, led by *Cesair*, " daughter of Bith son of Noah," who came to Ireland in the hope—vain, as the event showed —of there escaping the universal deluge. For two hundred years after that catastrophe, the land remained uninhabited, when one *Partholon* came with his followers, who in process of time were exterminated by a plague. Then came a certain *Nemhed*[1] and his people. Both Partholon and Nemhed were harried by sea-pirates called *Fomhoraig*[2]; from whom, indeed, the people of Nemhed suffered so much that they fled from the island, and some of them took refuge in Greece. There they were reduced to slavery, and once more, in a later generation, they escaped and returned to Ireland in three tribes, united under the general name " *Fir Bolg*."[3] After about a quarter of a century's domination they were subdued, but not exterminated, by a mysterious people called *Tuatha Dé Danann*, which means " The tribes of the Goddess Danu."[4] This people, by dint of skill in magic and in wizardry, conquered the island for themselves. They were not, however, left in undis-

[1] Pronounced something like *Nyev-ē*.

[2] Pronounced something like *Fōworai*. The sounds of Irish are so different from those of English that it is impossible to represent this exactly in English spelling.

[3] This name should be written thus, in two words. It is a plural, so that the form "Firbolgs," so often seen in popular books, is incorrect.

[4] This name also is much maltreated in popular books. The second word is often printed with a small initial (de) as though it were a French preposition, and the last name is often misspelt "Danaan." Though a genitive singular, it is often turned into an ethnical term, the people being spoken of as " The Danaans."

turbed possession. For they having slain a certain Ith, relative of a prince named Míl, who with his people had after many wanderings settled in Spain, the people of Míl (often spoken of in English as " Milesians ") came to avenge his death. Though the Tuatha Dé Danann strained all the resources of their magic arts, the druids of the people of Míl were too strong for them, and the sword completed what magic had begun. The Tuatha Dé Danann fled to the hearts of the " fairy mounds "—the ancient ghost-haunted tumuli that dot the land—and the children of Míl were left in undisturbed possession of the country, which, as the pious old chronicler does not fail to add, they will continue to enjoy *usque ad finem mundi*.

These traditions, as we have them, were compiled by a succession of historians living from about the sixth to the tenth centuries out of earlier material, the nature of which will be described in a later section. Wild though the stories seem to us, they were set down in all good faith by honest men, using the means at their disposal according to their lights. On the one hand they had the native traditions, some oral, some written, which had been handed down from the days of paganism ; on the other hand they had the infallible word of Scripture, and especially the chronology to be derived from its study ; and the task that they set themselves was the reconciliation of the one with the other. Their treatment of the first of these traditions, that of Cesair, is a good illustration of how they worked. In its original form, as various hints indicate, it was a flood-myth, such as has been preserved among many peoples and tribes (as for instance the story of Deucalion among the Greeks) ; and probably was once a tale, not of an antediluvian conquest of Ireland, but of the means whereby the world was re-peopled *after* the deluge. The historians were unwilling to reject a tale that ascribed so venerable an antiquity to the beginning of history in their country; but they could not accept in its original form a tale that so far contradicted Scripture as to assert that anyone except the people of Noah's Ark was saved from the waters. They therefore manipulated it so far as to (*a*) identify its flood with the flood of Noah ; (*b*) transfer its characters to the time preceding the deluge ; and (*c*) insert a bit of genealogy which brought the leader of the expedition, Cesair, into direct relationship with Noah.

There are a number of indications, which it would be impossible to discuss here, leading us to the conclusion that the stories of the invasions of Partholon, of Nemhed, and of the Fir Bolg are duplicates of one another ; and that under these various names we have different distortions of the native traditions of the aboriginal inhabitants. Of special importance in this connexion is the statement that the Fir Bolg were subdued, *but not exterminated* ; indeed the chroniclers enumerate a number of places in the country where communities of Fir Bolg remained down to their own time. This can mean only that in the time of the chroniclers there were people in the country differing from the dominant race in appearance, and possibly also to some extent in religion and in language ; and that these were rightly regarded as being survivors of an earlier population, who had been at some time conquered by the Celtic-speaking people to which the chroniclers themselves belonged. This is an ethnological *datum* of great importance, indicating the existence, in the early days of Christianity in the country, of a recognised strain of aboriginal blood.

In the foregoing paragraph it will be noticed that the earlier invasions alone are mentioned, and that the Tuatha Dé Danann are passed over. This " invasion," as will be seen later, is in a class apart, and its discussion belongs to a different section of this article. The story of the children of Míl is certainly what it professes to be : the tale of the coming of the Celtic-speaking " Irish " to their country, as they told it themselves. And, though here again it is impossible at present to enter into the demonstration, it is more than likely that the traditions of the Fomhoraig, who harried the aborigines, give us the story of the same event from the point of view of the people whom they superseded.

Among the points whereby these two strains were distinguished were certainly *stature* and *coloration*. For it is almost an invariable rule in the ancient sagas of Ireland, that kings, nobles, warriors, fair women, and, generally speaking, aristocrats, are described as being tall, and having blue eyes and fair hair ; while, on the other hand, persons in inferior position are usually described as short and dark. This convention is so regular that it cannot but have a basis in actual observation. It follows that the dominant conquerors, under whose auspices the ancient literature was systematised, were tall and fair, the subordinate aborigines short and dark. In some stories, it is true, we find a *dark* complexion regarded as the type of beauty ; thus, a common opening of folk-stories is the incident of a hero killing a raven on a snowy day, and vowing that he will never marry till he meets one with hair as black as the raven, skin as white as the snow, and cheeks as red as the blood. Such stories as these (the well-known tale of Deirdre is an example), in which *dark* hair is extolled, most probably originated among the aboriginal population. By such physical contrasts between the two opposing races many other details and incidents of tradition may be explained ; thus, we see here one of the roots of the many tales about Irish giants. The invading tall race appeared gigantic to the shorter aborigines, just as the well-nourished people of Canaan seemed gigantic to the stunted and half-starved Hebrew spies ; and the disproportion became exaggerated as the story passed from generation to generation.

The subsequent course of the history, as narrated by the native chroniclers, may be briefly set forth ; for we shall have occasion to refer to it in later sections. When the people of Míl established themselves in the land, the sovereignty was divided between Eremon and Emer (or Eber), the sons of Míl. After a year Eremon slew Emer in battle, and reigned as sole monarch. After his death his sons took the kingship, but they were slain by the sons of Emer in expiation of their father's death ; and from this onwards the kingship is involved, we are told, in an endless blood-feud between the descendants of Eremon and those of Emer. Each king reigns in virtue of having slain his predecessor, and is himself slain by his successor ; to this rule there are hardly any exceptions. Till we reach Cormac son of Art, in the third century A.D., the chroniclers can scarcely be said to narrate trustworthy history in the form in which they present it ; but doubtless much historical matter is embodied in their narrative, and the kings of which they tell no doubt had for the greater part an actual existence, not however necessarily as kings of all Ireland, but as chieftains over different tribes and territories. Various lines of evidence point to the conclusion that it was Cormac who established a monarchy over the whole island, with its seat at Temhair (in English Tara) in Meath—till then simply the residence of the local chieftain.[1] The reign of this Cormac is of cardinal importance for early Irish history. Two centuries after him came Patrick, who organised the Christian Church in the country ; and from him onwards the course of history is clear and well established.

THE ANTHROPOLOGICAL EVIDENCE

A few preliminary remarks upon the elements that constitute a *race* will be necessary to enable the reader to follow the particulars set forth in this section. We have to see whether modern scientific investigation enables us to confirm the evidence from the ancient traditions, or whether its testimony is contradictory.

Humanity can be classified according to various schemes, each of which is useful in its own proper place, but which cannot be confused without falling into grave errors. We may use such elements as religion, language, political relationship, social organisation, and physical character separately ; but never interchanged with one

[1] The name Temhair (in modern Irish spelling *Teamhair*, pronounced something like *tyawair*) means a conspicuous place, commanding a wide view. It is really not a proper name at all, but a common noun with this meaning, and there are several places thus denoted in Ireland ; they are distinguished from one another by adding the name of the district in which each stands, in the genitive case. Thus we have *Temhair Luachra*, the "prospect-hill of Luachair," a region in Co. Kerry. The full name of the royal seat in Meath was *Temhair Breg*, the "prospect-hill of the plain of Bregia." But as this was *par excellence* the principal "temhair" in Ireland, the distinguishing name is in this case usually dropped, unless for any reason there was fear of ambiguity.

another. Each of these bases of classification is independent of the others ; we cannot, to illustrate our
statement with an extreme case, classify mankind into
black people, Buddhists, Semitic-speakers, and so forth.
    Of these different elements that express the relation-
ship of a man with his fellows, only one group is constant
or approximately so. Men or communities may change
in religion, language, political relationship, and social
organisation to something diametrically opposite to
their former profession ; but they cannot change their
physical characters, at least not to anything like the
same extent, and not without a very long application
of modifying influences (such as climate, intermarriage
with aliens, etc.). A black man remains black whether
he continues in his native African religion or receives
conversion, or whether he continues to speak his native
language or settles in America or England and adopts
the language of his new surroundings. The division of
the people of the world into races depends *only* on
physical peculiarities. Race has nothing whatever to
do with language, religion, or any other element of
variation. The determination of the race to which a
community belongs is made by measuring or otherwise
observing the living people, or the bones of their dead
relatives or ancestors.
    This study, important though it is, has not yet been
carried out with anything approaching necessary fullness
in Ireland ; the anthropological study of the inhabitants
of the country can hardly be said to have begun. A
number of skulls from ancient graves, and a number of
modern living natives in different districts have been
measured ; but no materials sufficient for a basis for
generalisation has yet accumulated. The results here

F

set forth, so far as concerns Ireland, being based on the insufficient data which alone are available, can only be tentative.

In considering the people of Europe, three elements have been found to be of special importance ; stature, coloration—not so much of skin, which is almost universally white, as of hair and eyes—and head-shape. The last-named is determined as follows : the head (or skull) is measured from front to back, and from side to side, between definite points at the ends and above the ears, with a pair of callipers. The ratio between these measurements is then expressed as a percentage, by means of the formula $\frac{\text{Breadth}}{\text{Length}} \times 100$. The figure thus determined is known as the *cephalic index*. When the skull is broad, the breadth being large in comparison with the length, the index will evidently be a high figure, and when the skull is long it will be a low figure. There are several formulæ of classification of cephalic indices ; the simplest scheme, sufficient for most practical purposes, is as follows :—

Cephalic index under 75 : *dolichocephalic* (long-headed) skulls.
Cephalic index between 75 and 80 : *mesaticephalic* (medium-headed) skulls.
Cepahlic index above 80 : *brachycephalic* (short-headed) skulls.

The inhabitants of Western Europe fall broadly into three racial divisions. These are the Teutonic or Scandinavian in the North, distinguished by *tall* stature, *fair* colour, and *long* heads ; the Alpine in Central Europe, distinguished by *medium* or *short* stature, *dark* colour, and *short* heads ; and the Mediterranean in the south, distinguished by *short* stature, *dark* colour, and *long* heads. It is to be noticed that this classification depends not on the observation of a few individuals here and there, but on the average of a very large number of measurements that have been systematically taken in the different countries. It is further not impossible that the Teutonic is ultimately a branch of the Mediterranean stock, which has become bleached by long dwelling in a cold and sunless region, and that the parent stock of both colonised Europe from Africa, the majority of whose population is markedly long-headed ; whereas the Alpine stock is a wedge driven between the two from Asia, which is the great centre of short-headedness in the world.

So far as we can make any general statement, it would seem that the population of Ireland has been persistently *long-headed* from the first. There have no doubt been numerous short-headed individuals in both ancient and modern times, but always in insufficient numbers to upset the proportion. In this Ireland displays a contrast with England. For in England a short-headed strain became dominant at the beginning of the Bronze Age—in fact, it was most likely this short-headed people that introduced the bronze culture into England. They never found a footing in Ireland, however, and the bronze culture, which in Ireland advances *pari passu* with the corresponding civilisation in the neighbouring countries, must have been introduced by way of trade. The bronze-age people of Ireland are indistinguishable from those of the preceding Stone Age, and are most likely their actual descendants.

The archæology of Ireland belongs to another section of this work, and cannot here be discussed ; but it is necessary to indicate very briefly the evidence that archæology has to offer as to the peopling of Ireland in ancient times. We shall assume that the reader is aware that the history of civilisation is divided into three chief periods, called respectively the Stone Age, the Bronze Age, and the Iron Age, after the material principally used for tools and weapons in each ; and that, further, the Stone Age is subdivided into the Early Stone or Palæolithic Period, when man was still only a hunter, living on the produce of the chase, and the Late Stone or Neolithic Period, when he had learned the art of agriculture.

The leading antiquaries of Ireland are agreed that no trace of the existence of *Palæolithic* man has yet been found in Ireland. It has so far proved impossible to trace back the human occupation of the island further than the Neolithic period. The people that then made their way into the country—probably from Scotland— have left their traces in the chipped flints found at Larne and other sites along the coast, where hearths and other remains of early settlements have been found. Gradually they conquered the dense wolf-infested forests that cumbered the interior, and spread over the whole island.

Now this must have been the people that the ancient native historians call variously by the names of Partholonians, Nemhedians or Fir Bolg. The latter name is often used in modern books as a convenient term for the aborigines ; but its use is to be deprecated. It means absolutely nothing to modern science, and gives a spurious air of exactitude to our statements which unfortunately they do not as yet deserve. But if further research corroborate the results so far attained, that the stone-bronze people of Ireland were (1) short, (2) dark, and (3) long-headed, then they must be correlated with the Mediterranean European race. For this equation there is not wanting other evidence, and it may at least be adopted as a working hypothesis.

These people maintained intercourse with their brethren over sea, for we find innovations introduced elsewhere being adopted in Ireland : the erection of dolmens (see the archæological section) may be quoted as an example. The existence of these gigantic monuments in any country is of great anthropological importance : not only does it prove the existence of intercourse with other dolmen-rearing countries, from which the fashion was learnt, but also it indicates a high development of social organisation. The physical labour involved in erecting these structures, with cover-stones often weighing between 40 and 70 tons—in one case as much as 100—is sufficient to prove the existence of a spirit of co-operation that could result only from a sentiment of tribal unity.

The free intercourse with other countries, even in the Stone Age, to which these monuments bear witness, paved the way by which a knowledge of the use of metals entered the country, once that knowledge had been gained elsewhere. We find that even the primitive Copper Age had a footing in Ireland, and that a wealth of material is still extant for the history of the subsequent developments of the Bronze Age. Ireland having but little native tin, must to a large extent have depended on Cornish trade for her supply of that essential ingredient of bronze.

At what stage in the history the dominant fair-haired invaders found a footing has not yet been certainly ascertained : but it was most probably at the beginning of the Iron Age. It is just this period in the archæological history of the country that has been least completely illustrated by archæological discoveries, and we are therefore still much in the dark about the course of events and of cultural development. The newcomers were, like their predecessors, long-headed, and thus an important guide to distinguishing their remains is denied us. A people fair-headed, of tall stature, and with long heads must racially be regarded as Teutonic : the " Milesians " of Irish tradition, who conquered the rich gold-bearing land of Ireland, were simply forerunners of the Vikings, their relatives in blood, who in later centuries raided the descendants of the " Milesian " invaders.

Whenever this " Milesian " invasion took place, its result was that Ireland became the home of two peoples, totally different in race, and, at least at the beginning, in language, in religion, and in social customs. One of these people assumed domination over the other ; and all the legal institutions of the invader were framed with the express purpose of keeping the subject people in their place. While these elaborate enactments, some account of which is given below, were in force, intermarriage between the two races, the aboriginal so-called " Fir Bolg " and their Teutonic conquerors, was practically impossible. We may perhaps see a reflection of the condition to which the aborigines were reduced in their own traditions. As we saw in the previous section, they said that their ancestors had escaped from Greece, because they had there been compelled to work in slavery. The special work to which they were condemned was " carrying earth in bags of hide, from one place to another, so as to make fertile flowery plains of rugged mountains "—a statement that is unintelligible until we remember the hill-side agricultural *terraces* (dating as a rule from the Roman period), of which traces have been found in England and in Scotland. Walls are erected on the sides of mountains, and earth is painfully carried up and filled into the spaces intercepted between the walls and the sides of the mountain. Before the days of wheelbarrows the most probable way of carrying the earth would be in sacks of hide : so this story, wild as it is in its traditional form, nevertheless contains more than a germ of truth. From these bags the Fir Bolg (" men of bags ") were said traditionally to have derived their name.

Doubtless the institution of Christianity had some influence in mitigating the lot of the downtrodden aboriginal population, and the breaking down of the partition walls between the two castes. The racial distinction between them, however, lasted clear enough till the beginning of the extant literature, for, as we have seen in the preceding section, it was noticed by the early Christian historians. The final abolition of the castes must, however, be laid to the credit of the English. To these, the aborigines and their Teutonic conquerors alike were " mere Irish " : and the distinction once removed, intermarriage became less difficult, and the general racial type reverted to its original form, in accordance with the ordinary laws of race-inheritance. The modern native population is far more " Mediterranean " than " Teutonic," despite the many centuries of Teutonic domination, " Milesian," Viking, and English, to which the country has been subjected. In fact, it is most likely that the original " Milesian " stock has by now been bred out, people displaying Teutonic characteristics being of later introduction. As Ripley (*Races of Europe*, p. 332) has well shown, the national temperament likewise suggests a close comparison with the Mediterranean peoples of Southern Europe.

The next infusion that the population received was during the ninth century A.D. The Scandinavian sea-pirates found the rich monasteries of Ireland a tempting prey; and they forced an entrance on the country, founding settlements at the mouths of the chief rivers—such as Limerick at the mouth of the Shannon, Dublin at the mouth of the Ruirthech,[1] and so on. These intruders effected a permanent settlement: it is a popular error that they were driven out by the battle of Clontarf. Their adoption of Christianity paved the way for an absorption with the dominant classes even more complete than the fusion that had been gradually taking place between these and the aborigines.

It will be noticed that in these paragraphs on the very Celtic country called Ireland, no mention has been made of the *Celts*; and the reader may be tempted to compare the hackneyed absurdity of Hamlet without anyone in the title-rôle. This omission has been intentional, and will be rectified in the section on *language*. For the present the reader may be reminded of the elementary but often forgotten fact that race and language have nothing whatever to do with one another.

[1] Now miscalled the Liffey, a name which properly belongs to the region through which the river flows. The transference has taken place owing to the Ruirthech being often called *abha Life* (pron. something like "awa liffey"), "the river of Life [dissyllable]." The name "Annaliffey," often given to the waters of the river above Dublin, is a corruption of the intermediate name.

The fourth great influx took place at the time of the Anglo-Norman invasion, when the Eastern counties were peopled from various parts of England and Wales. The process of " anglicising " Ireland began at that time, and has been continuing ever since with varying success. In the sections on ancient geography, in the other volumes of this series, we indicate the main lines of the history of this process, so far as it is possible to compress it within the narrow limits at our disposal. The methods adopted for securing the desired result have been many and various. Legal proscriptions without number, of religion, social customs, native dress, language, even Celtic personal and topographical names : ridicule : bribes of money, rank, and other advantages : confiscation of lands and their compulsory colonisation by aliens : prejudiced education : all these and other devices have been tried to secure the impossible result of forcing into one mould two stocks which branched asunder in the Early Stone Age and which have been developing along their own lines during the countless centuries ever since. The chief result of these unscientific experiments (to call them by no harsher term), has been to produce some strange anomalies. Among these we may mention the survival of a dialect of mediæval English in two baronies of Co. Wexford, while on the other hand we may meet with peasants indistinguishable from their fellows in dress, habits, and language, speaking, it may be, no English, yet with totally un-Irish names. We may meet at any time in society a man with a name that links him with long generations of Irish chieftains, yet professing the utmost abhorrence and contempt for everything Irish ; or another whose ancestors were English a short century ago, and yet in all his interests and enthusiasms Irish to the core. This curious muddle is the direct result of seven centuries of misunderstanding.

ANCIENT SOCIAL ORGANISATION

We cannot doubt that the system on which the aborigines organised their society differed widely from that of their conquerors. Some facts respecting this obscure subject may be gleaned from known details respecting the *Picts* of Scotland and the north-east of Ireland, whom we may regard as a surviving sept of this ancient people. From these facts we learn that society was by them organised on a *matriarchal* basis. Descent was reckoned through the mother, not through the father; and kings were succeeded, not by their sons, but by their sisters' sons. This is a very primitive system, and with the advance of civilisation always in time gives place to the opposite system, in which descent is reckoned through the father (*patriarchate*). There are many hints and suggestions in the fragments of ancient Irish history that have come down to us of the former existence of a matriarchate throughout the country; indeed it is evident that the early historians were much puzzled by what seemed to them an anomaly, and laboured to invent explanations of some of the relevant facts which they recorded. It is noteworthy that all the famous assembly-places and palaces of Ireland — such as Tara, Emain · Macha, Tlachtga, Tailltiu, etc.—had traditions attaching to them ascribing their foundation or inauguration to *women*. This is so uniformly the rule, that it can bear no reasonable explanation except the assumption of a matriarchal organisation in the Bronze Age, when no doubt these ancient sites were first established.

For the conquerors we have, as might be expected, much fuller information. This is contained for the greater part in the legal tracts (published in six volumes under the name *The Ancient Laws of Ireland* in the Rolls Series) ; but the other branches of Irish literature, such as the romances and the saints' lives, give us most valuable information in addition. It is of course impossible here to set forth more than the outlines of the system on which society was organised.

The key to the understanding of the scheme lies in the conquest of the aborigines and their enslavement by their Teutonic successors. Elaborate precautions are taken to keep the subject people in their place, and to prevent any of them, by judicious marriage or otherwise, from obtaining a footing among the governing classes.

Our chief source of information regarding the castes of society is a tract of the eighth century, contained in the fourth volume of the *Laws* publication above mentioned. This document describes in order the rank, value, privileges, and (in the case of the lower orders) the disabilities of the various degrees of the community, beginning with the serfs and running upwards to the king. We learn that the whole body of the inhabitants were divided primarily into two classes ; the *daerchlanna* or serfs, and *saerchlanna* or freemen. The serfs had no rights : they were not permitted to enter assemblies or companies, nor were they entitled to compensation for injury to person or property. They could not give evidence, pledges, or oaths. Among them were included bankrupts, who had lost their freedom and all the privileges of their former class, with their property ; and small cow-tenders, loose livers, acrobats, and tramps. The obvious explanation of this enumeration is, that the aboriginal population were reduced to these humble means of making a livelihood. Bankrupts were counted among them, because, as we shall see, property was the chief qualification for admission to the upper ranks. It followed logically that a man who had lost his property had also lost the privileges that depended on his possessions.

Besides the serf classes there was a slave population (*mog* a male slave, *cumhal* a female slave, *fuidir* a sort of client occupying an intermediate position between slavery and independence). Slaves were classified as native or foreign, the latter being no doubt captured from the neighbouring shores of Great Britain in raids or warfare or by purchase. Giraldus Cambrensis (*Expugnatio Hiberniæ*, I. xviii.) tells us that the English of Bristol used to eke out their subsistence by selling their children as slaves to Ireland. St Patrick was in his boyhood one of these foreign slaves, captured in a raid. In some cases it would seem that slavery was imposed on criminals as a penalty.

The freemen were divided into the *non-noble* and the *noble* classes ; and the latter were elaborately graduated into ranks according to the amount of their property. The lowest, non-noble, element of the freemen was the class called *Fir Midboth*, an expression apparently meaning " men of mulct " ; but the meaning of most of the names applied to the ranks of society is quite uncertain. The Fir Midboth had no right to claim fosterage for their sons, and they owned no land ; but they could give evidence in a certain limited number of

ANCIENT SOCIAL ORGANISATION 93

cases, and were entitled to hold property in security. By increasing their possessions they passed automatically into the upper ranks, a possibility closed to the serfs.

The limits of the power of this and the other ranks to give evidence is a curious piece of relentless logic. Every freeman was entitled to compensation for injury. The amount of this compensation was graduated, not, as we might expect, according to the extent of the injury, but according to the rank of the two parties. The fine called *smacht* depended on the rank of the person paying the fine, and *eneclann* depended on the rank of the person receiving it. Whether *smacht*, or *eneclann*, or both together, should be paid, depended on the circumstances of the case. Now the *smacht* due from one of the *Fir Midboth* class was of the value of a yearling heifer ; this was the amount at which he was valued ; and it followed that it was not in his competence to give evidence in cases that involved a larger sum. The same disability applied to the upper ranks, each according to its own valuation. The rule was evidently framed to safeguard the interests of the rich, as most cases in which they were concerned would necessarily involve sums large enough to exclude the lower classes from giving their testimony. The same value limited the power of members of the different ranks of becoming surety and of giving bonds.[1]

The nobles (*aire*, plur. *airig*) were the land-owners, their rank being graduated according to the extent of the land owned by them. It is hardly necessary here

[1] In the *Laws* publication referred to above, vol. iv. p. cxcvi, the reader will find the privileges and disabilities of all the castes of society set forth in tabular form.

to enumerate the different grades ; they will be found in full in the table referred to in the footnote on page 93.

The whole body of residents in each district made up a *tuath* (pl. *tuatha*). This word is sometimes translated " tribe," which is not strictly accurate, as it would imply (what was not the case) that a blood-bond was recognised between all members of the *tuath* ; a better (but rather cumbrous) term is *population-group*, introduced by Prof. MacNeill. It is preferable to retain the native name throughout. Each group derived its name from that of *the ruling family* of the district. This name was expressed in various formulæ : these are of very different dates, and no doubt represent different phases in history, though the absence of records makes it impossible to trace out their mutual relations with completeness. Prof. MacNeill[1] enumerates the following types of "tribal" name : (1) Plural names, like the names of the Celtic tribes of the Continent : these most probably are survivals from the aborigines. Such are *Cruithni, Galeoin*, etc. ; (2) Collective names, in which the name of the ancestor is combined with various words as *dal, corcu*, or with suffixes as *-rige, -acht*, to denote that the family bearing the name are the " People " of the ancestor named ; and (3) *Sept*-names, wherein by the use of names denoting relationship (as *mac*, son ; *ui*, the modern O', grandson or descendant ; *síl*, seed ; *clann*, children, etc.) the connexion of the family with the ancestor is yet more definitely stated.

This division of the entire population into a large number of self-contained and self-governed groups prevented the rise of any full conception of *nationhood* in the

[1] *Transactions of the Royal Irish Academy*, **xxix.** p. 59.

whole community.   Till the coming of the English the mutual jealousies of the *tuatha* prevented any permanent fusion.   At all times a *tuath* was ready to seek the aid even of a common enemy if it thereby could gain an advantage over a neighbouring tribe ; much as Vortigern is said to have called in the aid of the Saxons in his own private quarrels with the disastrous result familiar to all.   So an Irish chieftain sought the aid of Agricola against some rival : so Brian leagued himself with the Vikings in order to put his great rival Mael-Shechlainn II. out of the way : and so at last a squalid quarrel between two chieftains paved the way for the entrance of the English.   A few far-sighted individuals, as Cormac mac Art, the founder of the kingdom of Tara, and the Mael-Shechlainn we have mentioned, tried their best to extend the interests of the people beyond the narrow boundaries of their own regions ; but their work was thwarted by jealous rivals, and was a splendid failure.

The unity and solidarity of the *tuath* was much enhanced by the ancient and very important custom of *fosterage*, which prevented the growth of a family exclusiveness, and absorbed the interests of the individual in those of his group.   By this custom a child, boy or girl, was not trained by the parents, but in the household of a " tribesman," who made himself responsible for the child's education.   The foster-parent took the child, in the most literal sense of the expression, for love or for money ; and if we may judge by the literary indications, the relationship between the child and his foster-parents and foster-brothers was as a rule closer than existed between him and his actual immediate blood-relations.   The institution was regulated by laws that contemplated every possible complication that might arise, and which made prescriptions accordingly. The fees payable varied with the rank of the parent and the sex of the child; the girl, being supposed to require more care than the boy, and being in later years less likely to be of service to the foster-parent, cost more than her brother. The child was delivered to the foster-parent while still a helpless infant, and remained till (*a*) his death, if he died a minor; (*b*) his marriage, which generally took place at the age of about seventeen; or (*c*) till he committed some crime for which the actual father disclaimed responsibility. The foster-father was required to feed and to clothe the child in a manner suited to its rank—the quantity and quality of the food and clothes due to children of different ranks was minutely regulated—and to educate him or her in all the accomplishments then deemed desirable; for boys, horsemanship, swimming, shooting, and chess-playing; for girls, needlework and embroidery. Children in the lower ranks of life were taught the various crafts suited to farm and home life—tending animals, wood-craft, and wool-combing, etc., for boys; grinding, baking, cooking, etc., for girls. Boys destined for an ecclesiastical, legal, or artistic career would naturally become inmates of the household of some noted master. A note that boys need not be taught swimming if there was no water near their home is interesting as illustrating the solidarity of the *tuath*; a man was expected to spend his life on the *tuath*-lands where he happened to have been born, and if such *tuath*-lands had no water, swimming would be a useless accomplishment.

This institution of fosterage and quasi-adoption must have had its origin at a very early date, before the growth of any conception of the family as a unit consisting of a single pair of parents with their children. In fact it prevented the growth of such a conception beyond a rudimentary stage. Family life was merged in *tuath* life. This however did not prevent the establishment of a strict individualism in property and also in legal obligations, which involved the interests of the nearest blood-relatives. The property of a deceased landowner was divided according to fixed rules among his nearest relations ; and the fines extorted for crimes and injuries were subscribed in stated proportions by the culprit and his relatives, and divided in similar proportions among the injured party and his corresponding relatives.

The fosterage system had some resemblance to the rules that governed the training of the young in Sparta, as laid down in the institutions that bear the name of Lycurgus. They had much the same effect—the breaking down of the natural family instincts for the benefit of the state or tribal community. They differed essentially, however, in that the Spartan system was artificial, imposed after the family individuality had developed, and devised expressly to destroy that individuality ; it could not, therefore, stand against the natural instincts of human nature. The Irish system, on the other hand, was a natural growth, developed in primitive communities, and overrode the same instincts by the irresistible force of ancient traditional sanction.

At the top of the scale of society stood the *ri* or king. The translation " king " is, however, not quite satisfactory, as it suggests in English the idea of solitary supremacy, which is rather foreign to the idea of the *ri*. The *tuath* chieftains were the earliest " kings," and

G

these kept the name even after it had acquired a larger significance. At some time still prehistoric, the separate *tuatha* had united into larger groups, in circumstances now unknown to us; and though the union was always loose and liable to temporary rupture and rearrangement it was nevertheless real, and a leader was appointed to rule over the groups thus formed. There were five of these, roughly corresponding to the provinces, into which Ireland is still divided, with the addition of Meath. Thus came into existence the *provincial* kings. Finally, doubtless with ambitions fired by the doings of the Roman emperors in Britain, the great third-century provincial king of Meath, Cormac mac Art, succeeded in extending his rule at least nominally over the whole of Ireland,[1] and in instituting the *high-kingship*, which lasted till it died with the death of Mael-Shechlainn II., A.D. 1022. Thus there were three grades of kings, *tuath* kings, provincial kings, and the *árd-rí* or high king; and this is fully recognised in the legal documents.

As we shall see in the section on Religion, the king of any grade was in pagan times an important religious functionary, if indeed he was not actually regarded as a god on earth. This (contrary to what might have been expected) restricted rather than extended his freedom and authority. He was subjected to a variety of prohibitions which were designed to safeguard his sacred office, and which cannot be explained in any other way. Some of these we shall note in the section referred to, as they more properly belong there; we may here note one or two of the legal requirements. A king was to be

[1] In point of fact Munster always challenged and resisted the suzerainty of the kings of Tara.

" full of law " (or perhaps legitimacy) ; he was not to lay his hand " on the three handles of a labourer " (the handle of a mallet, a shovel, or a spade) ; he must not travel anywhere alone, for his own protection—not only against assassins, but also against the tongue of slander, for it would be easy for an evil speaker to accuse the king of undignified conduct unless he had someone by him to prove his innocence ; and he lost his status if in battle he was wounded in the back.   It is an interesting illustration of the minuteness with which the ancient jurists contemplated all sides of a question, that they add to the last regulation a grim modification to the effect that the king did not suffer the penalty of degradation if the wound went through from front to back !

The property qualification was not the only passport to nobility.   Beside and parallel to the scale of rank depending on worldly possessions there ran two similar scales ; the one artistic, the other judicio-religious. The *poets* were graduated into a series of grades that strangely recalls the degrees of a modern university ; beginning with the *fealmac* or undergraduate pupil ; the *frisneidith*, " interrogator," and the *fursaintid*, " interpreter," who are to some extent analogous to demonstrators and assistant lecturers.   Next comes a rank poetically named the *sruth do aill*, the " stream from a rock," so called because " as a stream carries off loose rocks so that they become like the strand by reason of the heat of the weather, so this scholar "—this bachelor of arts, as we may say—" drowns bad scholars, whom he confounds with rocks of evidence and of common sense ; and he tempers his learning for the benefit of those of little education who would ebb before

men of higher ranks of learning."[1] It almost makes
one think of the young graduate who makes a little
money by University Extension Lectures! Next comes
the *anshruth*, the Master of Arts, and lastly the *ollamh*
or Doctor of Letters. His qualifications as set forth are
rather obscure, as we do not know the exact meaning
of many of the technical terms; but full expertness in
all the complex poetical metres was certainly one
requirement. The honour-price even of the student
was considerable, and the ollamh ranked as highly as
the highest nobles. In pagan times the Druidic, and
in Christian times the Christian hierarchy likewise
brought nobility to their members. The legal documents in their present form are written under the
domination of Christianity; and from them we learn,
among other things, that the offence of wounding a
bishop was so heinous that it was one of the few crimes
punished by death.

THE VALUATION AND TENURE OF PROPERTY

No coined money was in circulation in Ireland before
the Scandinavian kings of Dublin struck silver pennies,
which were at least partly imitated from the contemporary coins of the Anglo-Saxons. The only native
forms of currency in use were: (1) the precious metals,
chiefly gold, measured by weight, and either in ingots
or cast in the form of rings and bracelets; (2) cattle of
the cow kind; and (3) slave-girls. The standard was
the *set* (pronounced something like the English word
"shade"), which means literally "a treasure," but, in
estimating sums of money, denoted an animal of the
cow species. The derivation of the Latin word *pecunia,*

---

[1] *Ancient Laws of Ireland*, vol. iv. p. 357.

from *pecus* a flock, shows that this Irish system of currency was by no means peculiar to the country ; on the contrary it was universal before the invention of coinage, and it is fortunate that it survived in Ireland to so late a date that we are able to study it there probably more fully than anywhere else.

We have used the expression "animal of the cow kind" because the value of the *set* varies with the age of the animal ; and this introduces an element of complexity into the study of the Irish currency. Indeed, a sum expressed as so many *sets*[1] has no meaning unless we specify to which of several classes the *sets* belong. In the *Laws* this information is rarely given ; we must infer that this necessary branch of instruction was imparted *viva voce* by the jurists to their pupils, and the tradition is now lost. For example, we are told that a king paid 30 sets for the fosterage of his son. This must be a definite sum ; we cannot suppose that a law so precise in other respects merely said that the king paid 30 "treasures." The lawyers, however, knew what value to assign to the set in this and in other cases, though the knowledge is not recorded for us in any manuscript that has come down to us. If you asked such a lawyer what was the value of 30 sets, he could not tell you ; but if you asked how much did a king pay for his son's fosterage, he could inform you exactly.

The metals were measured by the *pinginn* (borrowed from the Latin *pecunia*), which could be subdivided into halves, quarters, thirds, and even fifteenths ; this is

---

[1] This barbarous plural, with the English suffix, requires an apology, despite the convenience of using it. The proper plural of the word is *séuti*, later *seoit* (pron. rather like *shōj*, but the exact orthoëpy cannot be represented in English letters).

enough to show that it was a weight, not a coin. The pinginn of silver weighed the same as eight grains of wheat. Three pinginns (proper plural *pinginne*) made a *screpall* (Latin *scrupulum*).

With regard to the sets, putting one passage with another, we find that the milch-cow (*lulgach*) and the plough-ox (*dam timchell arathair*) were each worth 24 screpalls. This was specially known as the *ri-set* or "royal set." A three-year heifer (*samaisc*) was worth 12 screpalls. This was the *set tanaise* or "second set," which thus was worth half the royal set. The third kind of set, the *set gabla*, perhaps meaning "two-fold set," consisted of a combination of two animals—*either* a yearling bull (*dartaid*, worth 2 screpalls) with a two-year cow (*colpach*, worth 8 screpalls); *or* a yearling cow (*dart*, worth 4 screpalls) with a two-year bull (*colpach*, worth 6 screpalls). In either case the third set was worth 10 screpalls.

For yet higher sums the *cumhal* (pron. *cūwal*, the *u* being nasalised) or bondmaid was the unit, and here again we meet with a considerable range of values. The normal value of the cumhal, however, seems to have been 10 sets, the set being further defined as being of the second class. The cumhal, therefore, was worth 120 screpalls. But in some passages we read of a cumhal worth 3 sets, and even only one; so that there is a wide range of uncertainty as to valuation in the absence of knowledge that was imparted traditionally.

A still higher unit is named in connexion with all the greatest money payments that the ancient documents have occasion to mention. This is the *secht-ccumhala*[1] or seven-cumhals, worth 840 screpalls.

[1] The doubled *c* in *ccumhala* has the sound of *g* hard.

An important application of these standards was to the valuation of land. Land was divided primarily into arable and non-arable, and these were further subdivided into three classes each, according to the good or bad qualities that the land possessed. The following was the table of length :—

3 grains	make	1 orlach (inch)
4 orlaige	make	1 bas (fist)
3 basa	make	1 traigid (foot)
12 traigthi	make	1 fertach (perch)
12 fertaige	make	1 forrach

On the basis of the *forrach* the larger land measure is calculated. A plot 12 of these measures long and 6 broad—a double square—was the *tir cumhaile*, the land worth a cumhal. Like most primitive systems of land measurement, this scale depended, for the smaller measures, on the average size of members of the human body, and for the larger on the size of the plot of ground that a team could plough in a given time. The Irish system differed from others, however, in assigning an apparently fixed value to the plot as so determined, irrespective of the quality of the land. The anomaly is, however, to be explained by the variableness of the cumhal and the set. To illustrate the system simply, we might say that in modern times it would be said that

x acres of good land is worth £m

x *plus* y acres of bad land is worth £m,

but in ancient Ireland it was said that

x acres of good land is worth 1 cumhal of many cows
x acres of bad land is worth 1 cumhal of few cows.

This *tir cumhaile*, however valued, was the unit of measurement, the ownership of which determined the rank to which the proprietor belonged. The *og-aire*, the lowest rank of nobility, consisted of those who owned one *tir cumhaile* of land ; and each grade from that upwards possessed a *tir cumhaile* more than the grade next below, till we reach the *ri tuaithe* or clan-king, owning a *tir secht-ccumhal*, or land worth seven cumhals.

The land as thus divided may once have been common property of the *tuath*, although traces of this stage are hardly to be found in the prescriptions of the *Laws* ; for when these were drawn up in their present form individual ownership was recognised as the normal principle of land-tenure. There were certain limitations on the rights of owners which derived their origin from the older system. The most noteworthy of these were framed to prevent an owner from so disposing of his land that it passed out of the hands of the *tuath* into those of another. Thus, land could not be sold (except to a "tribesman," and even then the rights of expectant heirs were carefully considered), alienated, or "concealed "—*i.e.* passed on to a son fraudulently adopted for the purpose of ousting the rightful heir. Moreover, a man was required to keep his lands in the same good order in which he got it, and to pass it on to his heirs with no greater debt, defect, or incumbrance, upon it than when he had received it from his predecessor. All the rules affecting land tenure show that the owner, so far from being absolute master of his property, was looked upon rather as the steward of the land entrusted to him for the benefit of the community at large.

On the land as thus held the owner had a tenantry.

There were two forms of tenantry, the relations between
which form one of the most complicated subjects treated
of in the legal documents.   We can here indicate merely
the broad outlines.   In both kinds of tenantry the
essential element of the contract was that the land and
farm stock was supplied by the landlord, and the labour
by the tenant, who paid a percentage of the farm produce as rent.   The primary difference between the two
varieties was that in the one (*saer-rath*) the tenant took
possession without giving pledges, merely acknowledg-
ing obligation to the landlord : in the other (*daer-rath*)
he was obliged to give security for the stock that he
held, and thus was much more tightly in the hands of
the landlord.   The rent was high : in the case of saer-rath
tenants the annual proportion was one-third of each set
of the farm-stock advanced, with an additional set at
the end of the third year ; that is, annually 33 per cent.
of the capital advanced and a triennial bonus equal to
the capital ; so that the landlord got his money back
twice over by the end of the third year.   The rent of
the daer-rath tenants was paid in food ; in fact it was
the daer-rath tenants who supplied the table of the
landlord ; and he could billet his friends on his daer-
rath tenants, or could come down with a party to the
tenant's house, and there consume the amount of food
due.   The tenant had (at least theoretically) the right
of refusal if in these billetings an amount of food larger
than what was exactly due should be demanded.   It
is perhaps questionable whether in practice it would be
possible for a poor man to get much satisfaction out of
a legal action against a rich man ; but there are on
paper a large number of provisions to safeguard the
tenant from oppression and the landlord from defalca-

tion, and to secure remissions and mitigations of the rent in such cases as the outbreak of a cattle-plague which destroyed the farm stock. Among these restrictions we may mention a remarkable provision that a debt due from the tenant to his landlord could not be inherited. The principle underlying this law was stated in the maxim *Marbaid cach marb a chinta*, " Every dead man kills his liabilities." It was considered that the chieftain was responsible for the defalcations of his tenant ; if he had not chosen to put pressure on him at the proper time, he could not claim from the tenant's heirs. On the other hand, if the chief had at the time of the tenant's death been pressing for payment, then the heirs were liable.

The tenants were subject to other liabilities, besides the high, not to say exorbitant, rent. The saer-rath tenants had to do a certain number of days' forced labour for the landlord. Both classes of tenants had to go a-hosting at the call of their chief ; daer-rath tenants paid a *smacht* fine for disobeying the call, while saer-rath tenants were condemned to double labour as a penalty. For desertion in battle, daer-rath tenants paid *smacht*, while saer-rath tenants paid *eneclann* (see above, p. 93). The higher the rank, the greater the fine, and the fine for desertion was as a rule greater than the fine for abstention, as to desert the chief in the midst of battle involved him in greater danger than to refuse to accompany him from the first.

It is not clear what causes determined the special kind of tenancy imposed on an individual. The meaning " free " and " unfree " which belong to the words *saer* and *daer* cannot be pressed too far, as though the daer-rath tenants were actually in servitude. On the other hand, there seems to have been a certain stigma attached to daer-rath tenancy ; we read of saer-rath tenants being reduced to daer-rath tenure as a penalty for crime ; and we find also that no one could voluntarily accept daer-rath tenancy except with the consent of his *fine* or family circle. In these and many other points we must await fuller light. The published edition of the legal tracts is in many respects unsatisfactory, the text being uncritically edited and the translation very faulty ; and some important texts still remain in manuscript. Till the whole is revised we must remain content with imperfect knowledge on many details of ancient Irish life. Indeed, it may be questioned whether Celtic scholarship is as yet far enough advanced to make a satisfactory edition of the legal documents at all possible.

THE LAWS AFFECTING CRIMES AND INJURIES

In modern law a distinction is observed between a crime against the state and an injury against an individual. To kill a man is a crime against the state, and is punished by the state ; to kill his dog is an injury which is punished by awarding compensation according to its value. In ancient Irish, as in many other ancient codes, both alike are treated as injuries to the person, and both alike are punished by awarding compensation to the injured party or his representatives. Further, the penalty is graduated less according to the nature and extent of the injury than according to the rank of the two parties involved, plaintiff and defendant.

The Irish law of crimes and injuries is a development and refinement of the primitive *lex talionis*, " an eye for an eye and a tooth for a tooth." In the early days of Irish society, no doubt, as among all savages, an injured person simply went and inflicted a corresponding injury on his assailant or a member of his family, with or without interest. But as civilisation advanced it was realised that some restraint and regulation of this primæval custom was desirable ; and by the time the *Laws* were drafted as we have them, this law of revenge had developed into a highly elaborate system of *distraint*, carefully planned to safeguard the interests of both parties. This was the normal method of redressing injuries of all kinds. The procedure was as follows : First the plaintiff served on the defendant notice (*apad*) of his intention to distrain. Then followed a number of days of grace (*anad*), varying in number with the circumstances of the case. If during this grace no satisfaction was given, the distress (*athgabáil*) followed. The plaintiff, in the presence of witnesses, went to the defendant's lands and drove off and impounded a number of his cattle. After the distress was carried out, notice of its completion (*fasc*) was served on the defendant. The goods remained impounded for a further space (*dithemh*), which like the *anad* varied in length with circumstances. During this period they were still the property of the defendant, and the plaintiff was bound to guard them carefully from injury ; if he neglected this and they suffered in consequence, the defendant could proceed against him. But when the *dithemh* had lapsed, the plaintiff had the right of forfeiting (*lobad*) at a certain rate per day, until a sum equal to the original debt plus expenses had been withdrawn. If more cattle than was due had been impounded, the balance was returned ; if less, the deficiency was made up by a fresh distraint conducted in the same way.

In the case of an illegal or unjust distraint, the defendant could either levy a counter-distraint, or appeal to the *brethemh* (judge, brehon), who tried the case, primarily, as an illegal distraint ; this seems from certain indications to have been the one form of crime that normally came into the cognizance of the courts.[1]   If the person appealed against were found by the court guilty of having levied an illegal or unjust distraint, he was fined 5 sets.   Claims for the possession of land were also heard by the courts, but not until the claimant had by a picturesque series of symbolic acts, whereby he typified his right to settle on the land, expressed his lawful claim to its ownership.   These acts, like the private distraint, were obviously survivals from the time when a man simply squatted on land which he coveted, and settled with a club the claims of any rival that might put in an appearance.

The procedure at such a court is unfortunately nowhere described : the ancient Laws of Wales give us much fuller information in this respect, and with their help, and scattered references in the literature, we can piece together something of what it must have been like.   It was primarily a popular assembly of the *tuath*, presided over by the *brethemh*.   That in pagan times it was strictly of a religious nature is quite obvious.   It was this connexion with religion, which must never be forgotten in studying the laws, that gave them their binding character.   Like most ancient codes, the Irish laws claimed to have been dictated by a god ; and though Christian scribes have been careful to expunge

[1] See, for instance, *Laws*, vol. ii. p. 52.

the actual statement, they have left enough to indicate the fact quite clearly. The administrators of the laws had thus at their back the terrors of the unseen world, and we can judge dimly what this meant who remember how the peasant of a generation ago feared to put his plough into fairy hills for fear of offending their supernatural guardians. The total absence of any trace of a police system, which has often been commented upon, is thus explained ; it was quite unnecessary.

LANGUAGE

A. *The Language of the Aborigines.* Nothing is certainly known as to the nature and affinities of the language of the earlier tribe or tribes that inhabited Ireland. Through the country there are certain place-names—especially river names—for which it is quite impossible to discover a Celtic etymology. These may preserve the memory of ancient and otherwise forgotten river-deities, adopted by the Celtic-speaking invaders and doubtless corrupted by their alien mode of speech. This corruption, the nature and extent of which cannot be estimated, makes it hopeless to try from an analysis of such place-names to arrive at some conclusion regarding the lost language. In Scotland, in the territory of the Picts, a number of inscriptions have been found, written in an unknown language, presumably that of the Picts, and most probably a dialect of the pre-Celtic languages of the British Islands. These inscriptions are unfortunately too short and too imperfect to afford us any information about its affinities. Bede and others preserve for us a few isolated words, which however tell us nothing.

The primitive language, whatever it was, became

submerged in the intrusive Celtic language. Our ancient historians, to whom we have already appealed for evidence as to the existence of recognisable aboriginal strains in the population of their own ·time, tell us that the early invaders of whom they narrate the traditions all spoke the " Scotic," that is the Irish language. This evidently means that the distinguishing marks of the aborigines was something other than language, and that by the time these historians wrote the pre-Celtic speech had been forgotten in Ireland, although as we have just seen a dialect of it survived in the remoter parts of the Scottish highlands till a comparatively recent period.

There are not wanting indications, however, that the loss of the primitive speech had not long taken place when written record begins. One illustration may here be quoted. The Irish name of the river Lee in Co. Cork is *Sabhrann*. Now in Ptolemy's geography, a second-century work, which gives us the earliest extant contemporary information about Irish place names, he tells us that the name of this river was *Dabrona*, and that the inhabitants of the city at its mouth were Ivernoi. This is probably one of many names for the aborigines. But how did Dabrona become Sabhrann ? The obvious explanation lies in a peculiarity of word-formation in Irish. In this language, as in Sanskrit, *so-* and *do-* are prefixes with opposite meanings, in which *so-* generally denotes a good or desirable quality, and *do-* its reverse ; thus *sochma* means " affable " and *dochma* means " surly " ; *saidhbir* means " rich " and *daidhbir* " poor " ; *sona* is " fortunate," *dona* " unfortunate." When Celtic speakers came to occupy a territory in which was a river called *Dabrona*, they would be very likely to slip the name into *Sabrona*, which, even if meaningless in their language, would sound of better omen in their ears. The evidence of Ptolemy seems to show that this change took place some time between the second and the sixth or seventh century ; and we thus obtain a hint of the time at which the Celtic language superseded the primitive tongue, whatever it may have been, of the Ivernoi in what is now the south of County Cork.

But how did a Celtic tongue find entrance into Ireland ? We have seen that the physical features of the dominant invaders link them with the Teutonic family. The Celtic languages seem to have developed among the Alpine race of Central Europe, of which hardly a trace is to be found in Ireland, though it is a conspicuous element in the population of England. There are two possible explanations. Either the Teutonic invaders, notwithstanding their racial connexions, had while still on the Continent adopted a Celtic dialect, and spoke it as their vernacular when they invaded the country ; or the language was imported from South Britain and other neighbouring countries by means of trade—being the language of culture, those who were obliged to traffic with the merchants for the desirable things of the Bronze Age were obliged to acquire and to speak it, as the Kerry or Galway farmer is compelled to learn English in order to bargain with cattle-dealers. Probably the former is the more likely explanation, in view of the way in which Celtic place-names are spread over the whole country, and the almost complete absence of Teutonic personal names in the traditions of the Invaders. The fact, however it is to be explained, affords a notable instance of the fallacy of confounding race and language together. There is indeed a considerable element of truth in the old paradox that England is a Celtic country speaking a Teutonic language, and Ireland a Teutonic country speaking a Celtic language. However introduced, the Celtic speech in time assumed a complete domination, which crushed out the older language altogether. As the tongue of the aristocracy, of daily life, of culture, and of religion, it had advantages before which its older rival could not possibly stand.

B. *The Celtic languages* are a branch of the Indo-European family, and are most closely allied to the Italic branch, of which Latin is the most familiar representative. Among their distinguishing characteristics must be specially mentioned the loss of the letter *p* from all words in the primitive Indo-European mother-speech into which that letter entered. Thus, in the word for " much " or " more," the primitive language must have had a *p* at the beginning, as is shown by such words as *plus* in Latin and πολύς in Greek, which are both derived from the primitive word. But the *p* has disappeared in all the Celtic languages. In Irish we have *il*, meaning " much, many " ; in Welsh *llai*, meaning " many " or " more." There are other peculiarities of syntax, etc., which distinguish the Celtic languages from their relatives in other branches of the Indo - European family, but this must here suffice.

The Celtic branch is further subdivided into two groups, the *Goidelic* (Irish, Scottish Gaelic, Manx) and the *Brythonic* (Welsh, Cornish, Breton). All these languages are still extant except Cornish, which died about the beginning of the nineteenth century, and Manx, which is now moribund. Among the marks of differentiation between these groups, the most obvious

H

is that the Goidelic branch retains the letter q in all words in which it is found in the primitive Indo-European, while the Brythonic language turns it into p. Thus the word for " five " was something like *quenque* in the old Indo-European. Goidelic has retained the original q sounds, though the letter q is no longer used in writing : in Irish the word is *cuig*. Welsh has transformed this to *pump*.

The branch which established itself in Ireland was the Goidelic. When first introduced it was a highly inflexional language very like Latin in construction. But it underwent a long and complicated series of modifications and simplifications as time went on, which can be traced to a certain extent by inscriptions and manuscripts.

A certain Scandinavian infusion must have been introduced into the country by the Viking settlements in the coast-towns, but little or nothing of it can be traced. It is singular that only two specimens of Runic writing have been found in Ireland.

There are not many traces of the Norman French language in the country, though it was introduced with the Anglo-Norman invaders ; at the same time English began to make its way in the country, and before long came to grips with Irish. As in all other points of difference between Ireland and England, the law was invoked to compel conformity with English customs. The most noteworthy Act was that passed in the twenty-eighth year of Henry VIII, which begins with these words :—

" The Kings Majestie our most gracious and most redoubted soveraign Lord, prepending and waying by his great wisdom, learning and experience, how much it doth more conferre to the induction of rude and ignorant people to the Knowledge of Almighty God, and of the good and vertuous obedience which by his most holy precepts and commandements, they owe to their princes and superiours, then a good instruction in his most blessed lawes with a conformitie, concordance and familiarity in language, tongue, in maners, order and apparel with them that be civil people, and doe profess and knowledge Christs religion, and civil and politique orders, lawes and directions, as his Graces subjects of this part of this his land of Ireland that is called the English pale doth, and most gratiously considering therewith upon the great love, zeale and desire, which his most excellent Majestie hath to the advancement of the state of this his sayde land, . . . that there is againe nothing which doth most conteyne and keep many of his subjects of this his said land in a certaine savage and wilde kind and maner of living, then the diversitie that is betwixt them in tongue, language, order and habite . . . his Majestie doth hereby intimate unto all his said subjects of this land, of all degrees, that whosoever shall for any respect, at any time decline from the order and purpose of this law, touching the increase of the English tongue, habite, and order, or shall suffer any within his family or rule, to use the Irish habit, or not to use themselves in the English tongue, his Majestie will repute them in his most noble heart as persons that esteeme not his most dread lawes and commandements."

The Act thus verbosely introduced is drastic, not to say Draconian, and contains provisions for penalising Irish speakers and for rewarding informers. If persecution could kill a language Irish would have died long ago.

But what Acts of Parliament could not accomplish has been partially effected in other ways. The great Famine of 1846-7, and the subsequent clearances and emigrations, have drained the Irish-speaking districts of their best blood. The inherent difficulty of the language makes it necessary for a learner to devote more time to it than most people can spare ; and ridicule, the material "gentility" associated with English, and a prejudice current in certain political circles that the Irish language is necessarily bound up with the politics of the opposing party, all hinder the efforts that have been made in recent years to check the process of decay, and thereby to secure for the country the many intellectual advantages of bilingualism. At best, even in many of the Irish-speaking districts, the younger generation now speak a kind of jargon, in which English words are mixed up with the Irish. In the other volumes of this series, details about the dialects and the present state of the Irish language are given.

LITERATURE

We confine our attention in this section to the native literature, in the Irish language. The works of Anglo-Irish writers, using English as their medium, do not here concern us.

According to Cæsar and other Classical writers, the druids (see the following section) were the instructors of youth in Gaul, and also in Britain, where their chief schools were situated. These writers tell us no corresponding facts about Ireland, but we know from native sources that the druidic system was established there also. The Gauls were able to write freely, as appears

from various facts that Cæsar records. The instruction
which the druids imparted to their pupils consisted to
a large extent of traditional poems, which were not
allowed to be committed to writing, but which were
learned off by heart and explained orally. We are
reminded of the sacred Vedas of India, instruction in
which was carried on in the same way. That the
druidic poems were of vast extent is shown by the
length of time which their study required—as much as
twenty years is mentioned.

Though the sacred poems themselves were never
written, there is sufficient evidence to show that writing
was practised in druidic circles. We are not to think
of vellum manuscripts, but rather of tablets of wood,
with or without a coating of wax upon them. Some
of the romances must have been committed to writing
about the beginning of the Christian era, because the
descriptions of weapons, etc., reflect the practices and
fashions of the time with an accuracy that we could
not explain if they had been passed down orally. The
alphabet used was the Roman. The language was Irish,
but not the Irish of the day. It was the literary Irish
of the old hymns, maintained artificially, as Sanskrit
was in India. The spoken language had long parted
company with it by the ordinary processes of linguistic
decay, and was now almost as different from it as Latin
is from French.[1]

Beside the Roman alphabet another, founded upon
it, was in use in Ireland. This was the Ogham char-

[1] Thus an inscription has been found in Co. Cork reading
Dalagni maqi Dali—(the stone) of Dálán son of Dál. In the
spoken language of the time when the stone was erected this
would have been *Dáldin maic Dáil.*

acter. It was a cypher, in which the letters of the Roman alphabet, in a peculiar order, were represented by a number of strokes, grouped around a central line. This character, there can scarcely be a doubt, was invented at first as an alphabet of finger-signs—like the deaf-and-dumb alphabet—and was originally intended as a means of secret communication. Afterwards it was adapted for writing short inscriptions, the fingers being represented by the strokes. Usually the edge of a standing stone does duty as the central stem-line. About three hundred inscriptions in the Ogham character are known to exist, and from these we have gleaned most of the little that we know about the Old Irish " literary " language.

The following is the Ogham alphabet as deduced from literary and epigraphic evidence. The five extra characters for vowels, at the end, are never found (with the exception of the first and, very rarely, the second and third) in lapidary inscriptions, but are given in MSS. with the value of diphthongs. Their real function is to de-palatalize adjacent consonants that would otherwise be palatalized, and *vice versa*: the distinction between the two methods of pronounciation of consonants being of great importance in the phonetics and the accidence of Irish, as it is in Russian.

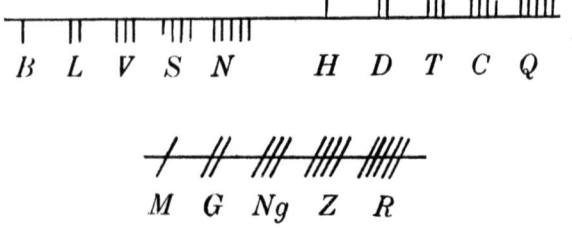

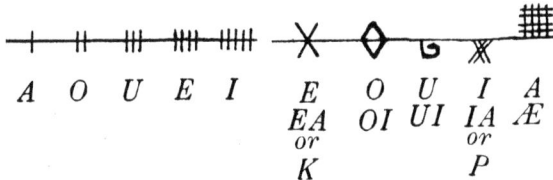

Christianity brought with it a knowledge of books and a new alphabet—the alphabet now called " Irish," but really an adaptation of the running hand of Roman manuscripts of the fourth century A.D. This alphabet is as follows:

ᴀ ᴅ c ᴅ e ꝼ ᵹ ɦ ɪ ʟ

a *b* *c* *d* *e* *f* *g* *h* *ι* *l*

m n o p ʀ s ᴄ u

m *n* *o* *p* *r* *s* *t* *u*

Under the auspices of Christian teachers a popular literature sprang up, founded on the old traditional romances, translated from the generally unintelligible literary language into the current speech of the time. In the process everything reminiscent of ancient paganism was carefully expurgated: this explains why so little direct information can be gleaned from the texts in their present form about the pre-Christian faiths.

Apart from the inscriptions, the oldest remains of Irish now in existence are certain glosses or explanatory notes, scribbled in the margins of biblical and other manuscripts in the Latin language. The earliest of these glosses date about A.D. 700. No manuscript wholly in Irish has come down to us from a date so early ; the oldest of these belongs to about the beginning of the twelfth century. But this manuscript was certainly compiled from earlier materials, and examination of the language of its contents shows that many of the pieces which it contains must have been first written down as early as the sixth or seventh centuries.

Considerably over a thousand manuscripts of Irish origin, dating from the seventh to the nineteenth centuries, are in existence : the oldest remaining being in Latin, but the vast majority after the twelfth century being in Irish. The earliest manuscripts are biblical or liturgical texts, but Irish is used in glosses and in occasional pieces from the beginning. The biblical manuscripts are often illuminated, those of the ninth century including some of the finest examples of illumination in the world.

The oldest MS. exclusively in Irish is the *Leabhar na hUidhri*, or " The Book of the Dun Cow," so called after the animal from whose hide the parchment on which it was written was said to have been manufactured. This great book was written at Clonmacnois, at least partially, by a scribe who is known to have died in A.D. 1106. It is preserved in the library of the Royal Irish Academy in Dublin. It is a compilation of romances, homilies, poems, etc., of a most miscellaneous kind. Among other important MSS. may be mentioned the Book of Leinster and the Yellow Book of Lecan in Trinity College, Dublin : the Book of Lecan, the Book of Fermoy, the Book of Ballymote, the Speckled Book, the Book of Ui Maine, and 23 N 10 in the Royal Irish Academy : Egerton 1782 in the British Museum :

Rawlinson B 502, Rawlinson B 512 and Laud 610 in
the Bodleian Library, Oxford.

From the Book of Ballymote

The general contents of this literature may be thus
summarised :

(1) *Histories and Romances.* These are: (*a*) native
traditions of the conquests of Ireland and of her
" tribal " wars, adventures of heroes, love-stories, and
other romances : and (*b*) translations and adaptations
of foreign tales of the same kind, such as the romantic
legends of the knights of Charlemagne, of King Arthur,
of the War of Troy, of Alexander the Great, Aeneas, etc.
These are both of great interest ; the first for the light
they throw on native manners, the second as illustrating
the relations of the country with other lands oversea.
Of the native tales by far the most important is *Táin
Bó Cuailnge*, the cattle-foray of Cuailnge—a description

of the great war between the provinces of Connaught and Ulster for the possession of the magical bull called Dond Cuailnge.

(2) *Theological Literature.* No early translation of any of the biblical texts into Irish is in existence, such as we have in Gothic and in Anglo-Saxon. There is, however, a large mass of ecclesiastical literature, consisting of homilies, lives of saints, rules of monastic discipline and of church order, Dante-like visions of the future worlds, prayers, etc. There are also a number of translations of similar texts from the Latin. In the later literature there are numerous poems of a didactic character, such as dialogues between the soul and the body, between death and the sinner, and the like.

(3) *Philology.* An interest in language for its own sake was traditional in Ireland. This probably has its roots in the druidic teachings and explanations which were necessary for the comprehension of the ancient sacred hymns of which we have spoken above. In the eighth century Cormac mac Cuilennain, king and bishop of Cashel, compiled an etymological dictionary of difficult and obsolete words in Irish : a work happily still extant and of the greatest importance for the study of the language, and full of valuable information as to traditions, etc. Even his faulty derivations are of value, as they sometimes throw light on the pronunciation of the words with which he deals. There are several other glossaries in existence as well as Cormac's, and in addition dictionaries of names of places and of people, telling the traditions about them, and the reasons for their names, as well as treatises on grammar and on prosody.

(4) *Science.* Under this head we include tracts on

astronomy, geography, medicine, etc. These are most, if not all, translations from Latin.

(5) *Genealogies and Annals.* Genealogies form an important part of the contents of the great manuscripts mentioned above. The importance of blood-kinship in determining a man's place in almost any system of society need not be emphasised, and that genealogies should be carefully kept is only what might be expected. These are of great historical importance. Of annals we have several collections, the most important of which are the *Annals of Ulster*, the *Annals of Inisfallen*, the *Annals of Tighernach*, the *Chronicon Scotorum*, the *Annals of Loch Cé*, and the *Annals of the Four Masters*. These give a succinct note of events, catalogued under successive years. Another collection, the *Annals of Clonmacnois*, survives in a seventeenth-century English translation only.

(6) *Legal Tracts.* Under this important heading there is an immense amount of matter, some of which has been printed in the volumes referred to on page 91. These documents, confused and unintelligible though they often are, are our most important source of information on mode of life and social organisation in ancient Ireland.

(7) *Verse.* Of this there is also an immense quantity. It must be freely admitted that the poetical value of the mass of verse literature is comparatively insignificant compared with its bulk, though there are many pleasing compositions, both ancient and modern. Much of the verse is merely mnemonic, being histories and genealogies cast into verse form to facilitate memory; and much else of it is hampered by the external elaboration of the verse forms. Some of these are almost miracles

of construction, but the poet has had to sacrifice free expression of his feelings to an adherence to the laws of alliteration and assonance by which he fettered himself. Nevertheless the study of Irish verse is of great historical interest. We can trace throughout a two-fold strand—the natural unfettered expression of the mind of the people in popular lays, and the more artificial productions of the literary schools in which, too often, sense is lost in sound. The study of the former branch of Irish verse can hardly be carried on apart from a parallel study of the traditional music, much of which has been collected, though there is still much to be gathered before it is forgotten ; for in this as in other things of tradition, songs learnt from books (often deplorable rubbish) are taking the place of the ancient memories. As an illustration of the complexities of the artificial metres we quote, by permission, the following imitation of one of them in English, by Dr Douglas Hyde :

> Tell of ancient times and men,
> the tale is told not often ;
> and to-day the dust lies thick
> on learned lay and lyric.

Here the following rules are observed : (1) there are seven syllables in each line ; (2) each pair of lines ends not so much with a rhyme as with an echo ; for the second rhyming word must have one more syllable than the first, so that the accent does not fall on the rhyming syllable in each line as it would in English ; (3) there is alliteration in every line—tell . . . times, tale . . . told, day . . . dust, learned lay . . . lyric ; (4) there is an internal rhyme between the last two lines—*and to-day* rhyming with *learned lay*. There are however many metres yet more complex than this.

RELIGION

It has been said in the preceding section that in translating the romances from the old literary language the references to the pagan religion were carefully expurgated. Happily this expurgation was carried out in an unscientific way, and in consequence many hints have been left us, from which we can piece together something of the religious beliefs and practices of the pre-Christian Irish.

The principles under which the christianising modifications were carried out seem to have been as follows: (1) When possible, tales about gods were turned into tales about heroes, the god being degraded to the rank of a "superman." The divinity of the gods could not of course be altogether forgotten, and thus we find that these degraded gods are still kept apart from the common herd of traditional heroes. The Tuatha Dé Danann, in fact, are primarily the pre-Christian pantheon of the official religion: and tales about them are to be criticised as tales about gods. This criticism must in *no* case be extended to heroes of the Celtic tradition outside the circle of the Tuatha Dé Danann. To argue that because Lug, an important personage of the Tuatha Dé Danann, was a god, therefore Cormac mac Airt or Cu Chulaind (who had nothing to do with the Tuatha Dé Danann) were also gods, is not legitimate. (2) When the first course was not possible, actions ascribed originally to gods were attributed to demons; as when Lia Fáil, the inauguration-stone that still stands on Tara Hill [1] used to scream at the

---

[1] That Lia Fáil is identical with the coronation stone in Westminster Abbey is another "vulgar error." The latter is purely Scottish and never was in Ireland.

inauguration of a legitimate sovereign. This was doubtless produced by a trick of some kind on the part of the presiding "druid"[1]: it was explained by those not in the secret as the voice of the god approving of his newly-ordained representative, and the explanation was modified by Christian scribes in the sense stated above. (3) When the action attributed to the god was beneficent, and could not be attributed to a demon, it was claimed as the work of the True God—as when the great law tract called *Senchus Mór*, which in its original form doubtless claimed the inspiration of some pagan deity, is in the Christianised form that we possess boldly attributed to the Holy Spirit. (4) When a god's name was casually introduced, as in oaths, it was simply excised, or vague sentences such as "I swear the oath of my tribe" substituted. The numerous cases in which persons are made to give the sun and moon, day and night, wind and rain as sureties must have originally been to the effect that the deities who presided over these manifestations of the powers of nature were called on as witnesses of the oath.

The problem of the ancient religion of Ireland is complicated by the stratification of the population. It is probable that the aborigines had their own religion, and that they maintained it at least in secret in the face of the official religion of their conquerors. There are a few scattered references that seem to hint at this, and further that it was, as we might expect, a despised and ridiculed faith.

---

[1] In an essay published by the Royal Irish Academy (*Proceedings*, vol. xxxiv., Sec. C, p. 231) the present writer has endeavoured to show that the sound was produced by means of a "bull-roarer."

Thus, we read that the serfs once revolted under the leadership of a certain Cairbre Cat-head. Though some obviously fabulous elements have attached themselves to the story, there is no reason to question the historical germ of the statement. This Cairbre, we are told, slaughtered the aristocracy, and made himself king. The result of this was disastrous; the earth withheld her fruits, the sea her harvest of fish; plagues and storms vexed the country, till the legitimate dynasty was restored in the person of one of the refugees from Cairbre's massacre. The importance of this alleged dearth during Cairbre's reign will appear presently : we are for the moment concerned with Cairbre's nickname, for which an old authority gives us several reasons, among them that " a cat was his god." This need not be taken literally : but it looks very like a specimen of the contemptuous things that might well have been said about the religion of the aborigines by their con- querors. It fits in, moreover, with other traditions about magical cats (of course the savage wild cat is intended) to which we find reference here and there. One of these cats was called *Baircne* ; and though the Christian scribes who report the little that we know about this animal have confused the traditions by foolishly identifying Baircne with the cat which represented its species in Noah's ark, they have pre- served enough to indicate that it held a very important place in pagan mythology, and very likely was originally an animal god.

As said above, the pantheon of the Celtic-speaking invaders is to be seen in the Tuatha Dé Danann, the race said by the chroniclers to have occupied Ireland just before the Children of Mil. Though the Christian writers have been at pains to reduce their divinity as far as possible, they have been unable altogether to blot out the "clouds of glory," which they trail fairly obviously. Among these gods are In Dagdae "the good god": Ogma (probably the *Ogmios* of Lucian), who presided over learning, and to whom was attributed the invention of the Ogham character: Diancecht and his son Miach, divinities of healing—and we learn that Diancecht was fabled to have slain Miach in jealousy because he proved himself the superior in the healing art, just as Apollo is said to have slain Æsculapius his son for exactly the same reason: we read also of Lug (or rather, perhaps, a group of divinities called by the generic name Lug) whose domain was the sun: a group of war-goddesses, to whom were affixed the names Badb, Macha, and Mór-Rigú (but these names vary to some extent in different texts): and numerous others, of most of whom nothing but the names are known. Above all we read of three mysterious brethren, called Brian, Iuchar, and Iucharba, of whom very little definite is told us, but who were of a divinity so refined that in a late text they are called the *gods* of this race of gods.

To extend this explanation of the Tuatha Dé Danann as gods to the other heroes of Irish romance and history has been stigmatised above as unauthorised and unscientific, though the latter have often been called "sun-gods" and the like, in accordance with a now obsolete scheme of interpretation of ancient mythologies, associated in this country with the name of Prof. Max Müller. The most that we can say for such an interpretation is, that, in the process of transmission of stories about the historical heroes, the tales have become contaminated with tales properly belonging to the gods,

which does not belong to them, and which as a rule is
easily dissociated from them. There is no trace of the
worship of these historical heroes, but the vigilant eye
can easily detect traces not wholly effaced of the worship
of the Tuatha Dé Danann. Thus, we read in the life
of the seventh-century saint Colman mac Luachain,
how a certain king was travelling with his jester, and
they had occasion to leave their horse tethered. The
king put his horse under the protection of the Christian
saint, and found it safe on his return. The jester, who
was evidently still a pagan, put his horse under the
protection of Oengus, and naturally found it stolen
when he came back for it. Oengus was a pre-Celtic
hero, probably a historical character, deified after his
death, whom the incoming invaders naturalised in
their pantheon by affiliating him to In Dagdae.

Besides these gods, one very important divinity must
not be passed over—the reigning king. For various
lines of evidence indicate that like the Egyptian Pharaohs
the king for the time being was regarded as the incarna-
tion of a divinity. The earth refused her crops when
Cairbre seized the sovereignty—for the god could not
condescend to tenant the body of so base a person, and
so while he (Cairbre) sat on the throne the god was
absent from his people. On the other hand, one of the
chief signs of a " good " king was extreme fertility,
calm weather, dew watering a land unvexed by heavy
rain-storms, and other like palpable evidences of the
favour of the divinity. By various rites, differing in
different districts, the king of the territory was inaugurated. Thus at Tara, he had first to squeeze
between two standing stones, reputed to mark the

I

grave of ancient druids called Blocc and Bluicne.[1] If he failed to do this he was rejected. He next was led up to *Lia Fáil*, and stood upon it. It would be impossible to stand upon it now, for it is standing erect ; but that has only been since 1798. The stone screamed under his feet if he was legitimate, and kept silence if not. The probable explanation of this phenomenon has been given above. In another part of the country —Tir Chonaill, the modern Donegal— an equally primitive and far more savage survival was practised : and in spite of the passionate denial of Keating, there can be no doubt whatever that the rite took place substantially as recorded by Giraldus. Here the candidate came before the folk on all fours, being led in with a white mare. The mare was killed, cut in pieces and boiled, and a bath filled with the blood. The new king sat in the bath and ate of the flesh of the mare and drank of the blood in which he was sitting ; the people also partook of the flesh. This simply means that the folk dwelling in that part of the country had the horse for their totem : their chief was identified with the horse and acted as a horse, and at his inauguration the life of the horse was infused into him by the mare's blood which he drank, and in which he bathed. Finally, the strange fact that so many kings met their death at the hands of their successors in itself points to the divinity

---

[1] This is the evident explanation of the confused tale that the chroniclers tell us, writing as they do after these customs had been abandoned and were beginning to be forgotten. They say that the king was led up to the stones *which closed before him* if he was not legitimate, and opened out before him if he were the lawful sovereign. Comparison with practices well-known in other parts of the world make it clear that what really happened was as described above.

of the king. The man in whom the god condescended to dwell must be strong and vigilant ; when he relaxed so as to let himself be killed, he was no longer fit for his high office, and a stronger than he took the sovereignty.

If there is little information available on the nature of the gods, there is still less regarding the rites of worship. We have hints of sacrifice, including human sacrifice ; processions, in a circling path, probably imitating the circling course of the sun ; oracle-giving and divination ; the custom of depositing votive gifts ; the observation of sacred times and seasons ; periodical assemblies, which combined the functions of religious gatherings, markets, deliberative assemblies, and meetings for sports and games ; and the propitiation of the *manes* of the dead by elaborate burial rites. The chief sacred seasons were *Beltene*, the first of May—the beginning of summer ; *Samain* the first of November—the beginning of winter ; and *Lug-nasad* a festival in honour of Lugh, at the beginning of August ; the chief assembly places were *Carman*, in Kildare, *Tlachtga* near Athboy, *Tailltiu*, now Telltown in Meath, *Uisnech* in Westmeath, and *Tara*. But probably periodical assemblies on a smaller scale took place round the grave-mounds of all noted heroes.

Among the elements of the pagan religious life of the country we cannot omit to notice the institution of *gessa* or prohibitions. Some of these were personal, others belonging to rank or office. Thus the king of Ulster was forbidden to attend an assembly at a place called Echrais Ratha Line ; to listen to the flutterings of birds of Linn Sailech ; to celebrate the feast of the flesh of the bull of Daire ; to go on Magh Cobha in the month of March ; or to drink of the water of Bo Neimhid during the daytime. It so happens that this series is easily explained, at least in part. The assembly, and the feast of the bull were obviously religious ceremonies from which for some reason the divine head of the province was excluded—most probably because they were *aboriginal* festivals, and therefore of an alien religion : the flutterings of birds are equally obviously an oracle : some uncanny influence hurtful to royalty was abroad in Magh Cobha in March : and the well of Bo Neimhid was a sacred well whose guardian spirit would also be injurious. But there are other taboos that are not so easily understood, and that must have their origin in events of which no other record is preserved. For example, the king of Connaught was forbidden " to contend in running with the rider of a grey one-eyed horse at Ath Gallta between two posts."

The mediators between gods and men were the *Druids* (Irish *drui*, Nom. Plur. *druid*). The Druids of Ireland were no doubt dignified functionaries, similar to those of Britain, and of the Continent ; Cæsar speaks of the latter with undisguised respect. We learn from his oft-quoted description that the Druids were (1) the priests, who presided over sacrifices ; (2) the repositories of learning and the instructors of youth ; (3) the advisers and directors of the community at large. Their learning was stored in the sacred poems to which we have already made allusion ; these never having been committed to writing have been lost. If they were not above a bit of " mystification "—like the screaming of the stone on Tara—they were no worse in this respect than other ancient priesthoods. In the later Roman writers the lurid and sensational side of druidism (which no doubt had a real existence) is emphasised. This is quite intelligible. It was to the interest of the Roman writers to blacken as much as possible the people whom they subdued. The human sacrifices which they describe with a wealth of hideous detail were most likely exceptional, dictated by the pressure of extraordinary catastrophes ; and naturally, the more the Romans had to do with a country the more frequent became the apparent necessity for such exceptional rites. But these later writers have coloured our own popular histories, and in consequence most people have an idea that Druids were people who spent their time cutting mistletoe, and burning people alive in wicker crates.

In the extant Irish literature the Druids have suffered in another way. The Christian adapters have taken advantage of the unfortunate fact that another word, very similar in form but not connected with the name of the priestly caste, *druth* to wit, means a profane jester. The Druids accordingly appear as jugglers and vulgar buffoons, and are put in all kinds of undignified positions. Very careful criticism has to be applied to all the information that we have about the Druids and their functions and doings before we can be said to have a clear idea on these obscure subjects.

THE CONVERSION OF IRELAND TO CHRISTIANITY

The beginnings of the conversion of Ireland are no longer to be traced. The leaven of Christianity was working among the Romanised Britons by the end of the second century, and it is not improbable that some of its influence may have crossed the Irish Sea. There is an ancient tradition that King Cormac who died,

according to the annalists, in A.D. 266, had imbibed
some rudiments of Christian teaching before his death.
This is not impossible ; his history shows that he was
greatly influenced by the events which took place in
his time in the sister island.　There were in any case
Christians in Ireland at the beginning of the fifth century,
for Palladius as we learn was sent in A.D. 431, by the
pope on a mission to "the Scots" (*i.e.* the Irish) that
believed in Christ.　Palladius proved a failure (or died ?),
and in the following year Patrick arrived to take up
his work.　To Patrick's immense energy and power of
organisation is due the successful establishment of the
Christian Church in Ireland.　The victory was, however,
by no means so bloodless or so complete as his enthusiastic biographers loved to make out.　Paganism endured
after St Patrick, and we have several hints that the
struggle between it and Christianity was not without
severity.　The drastic modification of the literature is
one of these indications.　Another lies in the nicknames
by which the deities of the opposing religions were
reviled.　The chief god of the pagans was called *Cromm
Cruaich* or *Cenn Cruaich* "the gory crooked one" or
"gory-head"; his worshippers retaliated by giving the
sacred Figure on the Crucifix a scurrilous name that
still survives in modern folk-tales, the narrators of
which are blissfully ignorant of its original application.
Coarse tales were invented and told about the rival
deities ; a remarkable specimen of these is the story
called *The Second Battle of Moytura*, preserved in a
manuscript in the British Museum.　We have seen that
down to the seventh century, or two hundred years
after St Patrick, there is evidence that Oengus-worship
was not dead.　It has indeed often been suggested that

the fairies of modern superstition are really the old gods, still remembered. This is however doubtful: it is impossible to trace much resemblance between the statements made as to the supposed nature of the modern fairies, and the recorded facts concerning the Tuatha Dé Danann. There is little or no evidence in ancient Celtic literature for a belief in beings similar to the fairies of modern days, and perhaps that they are pre-Celtic in origin—the problem still awaits solution.

THE RELATIONS OF IRELAND WITH FOREIGN COUNTRIES

Even by the beginning of the age of Bronze the inhabitants of Ireland had established relations with the countries oversea. The improvements in weapons, etc., that were introduced here and there were learnt and adopted in Ireland as well. Ireland having but little native tin, insufficient for the requirements of the Bronze Age, a trade with tin-bearing regions had to be established if any progress was to be made at all. On the other hand, the stores of native gold in Ireland made Ireland a country with which it was desirable to trade.

Coming down to the Iron Age, and the period of historical record, we find Ireland having connexions with oversea countries in three ways ; by commerce, warfare, and colonisation.

1. *Commerce.* The evidence for ancient Irish commerce has been studied by the late Prof. Zimmer. The most important trade was the traffic in wine with Gaul. Wine, which could not possibly be produced in the climate of Ireland, appears at the court of Ailill and Medb, the king and queen of Connaught in the first century B.C., and about the same time in the house of

Bricriu, situated over Dundrum Bay.　Later, in A.D. 533, Muircertach, king of Ireland, like the Duke of Clarence, was drowned in a vat of wine.　But even before his time, in the second century, the Alexandrian geographer Ptolemy shows an extraordinary knowledge of the capes, inlets, islands, and other geographical features of the coast-lands of Ireland, and of the tribes dwelling on the shore.　Indeed, he knows Ireland at least as well and as fully as he knows Britain, though the latter island had been directly under a Roman domination which never extended to Ireland.　This knowledge must have been acquired from merchants.　It is commonly supposed that all trade and all immigration must have made their way into Ireland over England ; but this is by no means necessary, and is indeed opposed to fact. St Patrick's *Confessio* tells us of the trading ship from Ireland to Gaul in which he escaped from his servitude. In Adamnan's *Life of St Columba* we find news of an earthquak in Italy being carried by Gaulish sailors to Iona within a few months of its occurrence ; in the life of St Ciaran (died A.D. 542), we hear of Gaulish wine-merchants who sailed up the Shannon as far as Clon-macnois in the very heart of Ireland ; and in the life of St Columbanus, at the beginning of the following century we learn that there was a merchant ship accustomed to ply between Nantes and Ireland.　Under the date 1130 the Irish annals record an incident which teaches us that Cork, Lismore, and Waterford were then trading ports ; and finally Giraldus Cambrensis, who was in Ireland in 1186, describes the Irish of his time as carrying on an active trade in wine directly with French ports.

　　2. *Warfare.*　There are several references to foreign

conquest or domination in the time of ancient kings. It is very hard to say what lies at the base of such stories. Thus we are told that Ugoine the Great ruled over half Europe at a date some 500 years before the Christian era. This is very likely an Irish echo of the Gaulish legend of King Ambigatus, of which Livy preserves an abstract. Again, Crimthann (A.D. 9, according to the annalists) is said to have led a plundering expedition to the coast of Wales, and brought back much booty. This is, not improbably, essentially true : Crimthann, whatever his true date may have been, was a historical character, and the site of his fortress on the promontory of Howth, near Dublin, still bears his name. Then Nathi is said to have been killed by lightning in A.D. 428 when on a hosting to the Alps. This is probably a mistake of the later chroniclers, who mistook the name of some Irish mountain for *Sliab Ealpa*, the Irish name for the Alps.[1] The great Cormac does not seem to have carried his conquests beyond the shores of Ireland, for a tale that brings him on a warlike expedition to Scotland is most probably legendary. His great-great-great-grandson Niall was, however, more enterprising, and there seems no reason to doubt that he led an expedition over sea, and even measured his strength against the

---

[1] Such confusions of name are a fruitful source of error and false historical interpretations. Another probable example may be here noticed. The historians say that the Gaelic people are descended from a princess named Scota, daughter of " Pharaoh, king of Egypt." This is probably based on some tradition about a king (or a god) bearing the *Pictish* name of Forann, which happens also to be the form that the name Pharaoh assumes in Irish texts. The original story was most likely a saga of the beginnings of intercourse between the aborigines and their Celtic-speaking Teutonic conquerors.

might of Rome.   The accounts of the expedition that
we possess are confused, and it is evident that the
chroniclers had never a very clear idea of what really
happened.   They carry Niall to the Loire and even to
the centre of Europe ; but the adventure can hardly
have happened anywhere but in South Britain.   The
result was disastrous, and Niall was slain.

3. *Colonisation*.   We read of no further attempt to
carry military expeditions over sea ; an Irish chieftain
had enough to do to keep himself guarded from rivals,
and later from the Viking and Anglo-Norman hordes,
greedy of gold and of land.   But on the opposite coasts
parties of settlers, driven by oppression from their
homes, found a footing on the shores across the Irish
Sea.

The most important of these was the tribe of the
Dessi.   This was originally a semi-savage half-nomadic
clan, quartered in the neighbourhood of Tara ; the name
of the Barony of *Deece* in Meath still preserves their
tribal name.   A libertine son of King Cormac wronged
a daughter of the chief of the Dessi, and he came up to
avenge the injury.   In the struggle Cormac lost an eye,
which disqualified him from reigning any longer : one
with a personal blemish being forbidden to reign as
king.   He therefore abdicated in favour of his son
Cairbre, who, to revenge the injury done to his father,
drove the Dessi out from the lands on which they
had been settled.   They made their way southward,
to the present Co. Waterford, and remained there long
enough to affect the local nomenclature of that part
also of the country ; for in the two baronies of *Decies*
we again see a trace of this people.   A branch of the
clan subsequently crossed over to South Wales shortly

after, *i.e.* during the third century. The numerous inscriptions with Goidelic names, found in Wales, are probably tangible memorials of this colonisation.

The Irish colonisation of Western Scotland, whereby the name of Scotia passed ultimately from Ireland to Scotland, is an important event that cannot be passed over. The true history of this event is obscure, like that of so many other important events in the early history of the British Islands, owing to the scantiness of the records and their lateness as compared with the period of the events themselves. Somewhere in the second quarter of the fourth century a raid on an extensive scale was made by the monarchs of Meath on the south of the province of Ulster. This had the effect of crowding the Ulstermen up into the corner north and east of Lough Neagh—the region then called Dal Riada, but now Co. Antrim. Finding this too strait for them, they were compelled to cross the sea into North Britain. Shortly after this time, in A.D. 360 we begin to hear of the *Scots* (*i.e.* Irish) as leaguing with the Picts in raiding the Northern borders of Roman Britain. These Scots, who now appear in Roman history for the first time, were most likely settlers from the northern regions of Ireland. Though these first Irish colonists in Scotland seem to have been driven back to their native country by the Romans, they returned, and a stream of emigration was inaugurated which culminated, in the sixth century, in the establishment of the Dalriadic kingdom of Argyll.

Under this heading also we should notice the monastic colonies which penetrated from Ireland to many parts of the Continent, and even so far afield as Iceland. This missionary enterprise began with the settlement of

Colum Cille (Columba) in the Island of Iona, A.D. 563
The long series of Irish missionaries to the continent of
Europe begins with Columbanus, born in 543, who
laboured in Burgundy, Switzerland and Northern Italy.
Among many others who carried the gospel to different
parts of the Continent in succeeding centuries may be
named Fursa, Fiachra (from whose name the French
word " fiacre " is derived), Colman, Cathal (from whom
San Cataldo on the coast of Otranto in the " heel " of
Italy is named). It is interesting to note that the
earliest remains of the Irish language now extant, with
the exception of the meagre inscriptions in the Ogham
character, are the glosses written in the margins of their
Latin manuscripts by these missionary monks. By far
the greater number of these precious linguistic relics are
in libraries on the Continent, some of them, such as
those at St Gall in Switzerland, being still preserved in
the monastery where they were first written by
missionary monks of the eighth and ninth centuries.
The missionary enterprise of the Irish Church did not
cease till the eleventh century, when we find the famous
anchorite Marianus Scotus (Mael-Muire) at Ratisbon.
These travellers not only carried knowledge abroad ;
they learnt many things in the countries to which they
went, and no doubt were the medium of communicating
a knowledge of them to Ireland. Improvements in
architecture which we can trace about this period of
missionary enterprise are probably at least partly to be
ascribed to the influence of monks returned from abroad.

A NOTE ON THE LAND DIVISIONS OF IRELAND

The divisions of Ireland are different in some respects
from those of England, as a consequence of their being

monuments of English administration grafted upon the ancient native systems. The country is divided into (i) *Provinces*, a native division, derived from the ancient pentarchy. These provinces were maintained for ecclesiastical purposes after the coming of the English, and continued to be five in number till Meath was incorporated with Leinster in the reign of James I. The provinces are divided into (ii) *Counties*, modelled on the English counties, and entirely English creations. The formation of the counties has been a long process, begun in the reign of King John, and not completed till the seventeenth century.

The *shiring* or division of a country into shires for judicial administration by a sheriff (shire-reeve) was an essential preliminary to its administration according to English forms ; the progress of the work of shiring is therefore a mirror of the progress of the work of Anglicising it. On that account we give, in the volumes devoted to the several provinces, the dates of the shiring of each so far as they can be ascertained.

The counties are divided into (iii) *Baronies* which more or less correspond to the ancient *tuath* lands, and often bear the name of the *tuatha* which were their rightful owners. The name " barony," however, is a relic of the English confiscations of tribal territories. Shortly after the arrival of the English, De Lacy to whom the kingdom of Meath had been granted, parcelled it out among subordinate barons, to hold in feudal subordination to himself. To these subordinate divisions the name " barony," was given, and the name gradually extended to other counties. The Baronies are divided into (iv) *Parishes*, a division based again on ancient *tuath* territories, but made for definitely ecclesiastical purposes about the twelfth century ; and finally the Parishes are divided into (v) *Townlands*, which represent, probably, the most primitive unit of land-division, the homestead, and are thus the oldest divisions of all. The English village community is an institution quite foreign to Ireland ; in England the church is the centre of what is to all intents and purposes a miniature town, and the fields between the villages are often singularly bare of houses ; in Ireland the people are scattered, each family on its own holding, and except for a few shops, schools, and the parish clergy house, there is not much concentration of population save in the various county and market towns.

NATURAL HISTORY

IF one were to draw a section across land and sea from France or Belgium through England and Ireland, and on for a few hundred miles into the Atlantic, it would be realized that these islands are strictly a portion of the European continent, and that a very slight alteration in the relative level of land and sea would connect them with the mainland. Compared to the depth of water covering the ocean floor, the merest film extends between France or Germany and England, and between England and Ireland, and continues for some distance westward to the edge of the continental shelf, where the ground drops somewhat abruptly into the abysses of the Atlantic. There is ample geological evidence of fluctuations in the relative level of land and sea within comparatively recent times, and there can be no doubt that the bulk of the animals and plants which inhabit our islands migrated into them over land-surfaces since sunk below the sea. The fauna and flora of Great Britain resemble those of the adjoining parts of the Continent, but on a reduced scale as regards variety : many species would appear never to have spread so far westward, or perhaps they arrived at the present limit of the mainland after the breakdown of the connecting bridge ; while others which entered our countries may have since become extinct under the more rigid conditions of insular life.

Just as the fauna and flora of Great Britain resemble those of West Europe on a reduced scale, so those of Ireland represent the fauna and flora of Great Britain in a reduced degree. Many species of plants and animals familiar to the English naturalist are to be sought in vain in Ireland. The fact that a number of these have a wide range in Great Britain, and exist there under a considerable variety of conditions, points to the conclusion that these species never arrived in Ireland, since if they had, in all likelihood they would have succeeded in establishing themselves there also. This makes it seem probable that the English-Irish land-connection broke down before the English-Continental one, so that although able to enter and colonize England, these species found their way to Ireland already barred by the Irish Sea. The suggestion that many entered Ireland and afterwards became extinct is rendered unlikely by the fact that up to the present remains of few of them have been discovered in peat-bogs, bone-caves, or other similar places where the relics of past generations of animals and plants are found entombed. Among the English animals which are thus missing in the Irish fauna may be mentioned the Polecat and the

Weasel, the Mole and the Voles, the Roebuck and the English Hare, and all the British Reptiles and Amphibians except the Brown Lizard, the Natterjack Toad, the Common Newt, and the Common Frog. Among plants we miss such familiar English species as the Needle Furze (*Genista anglica*), the Common Rock-rose (*Helianthemum vulgare*), Sweet Milk-Vetch (*Astragalus Glycyphyllos*), Small Marsh Valerian (*Valeriana dioica*), Black and White Bryonies (*Tamus communis, Bryonia dioica*), Lily of the Valley (*Convallaria majalis*), Spurge Laurel (*Daphne Laureola*), Daffodil (*Narcissus Pseudonarcissus*), and Mistletoe (*Viscum album*). This reduction in variety of animals and plants along with reduction of surface in insular areas is a familiar feature to the student of geographical distribution.

A fact of much greater significance emerges when we find that in Great Britain there are certain forms of animal and vegetable life which are not found on the adjoining continental lands. And our interest is keenly aroused when we discover that this peculiarity is much more pronounced in the fauna and flora of Ireland, where certain animals and plants, some of them abundant and conspicuous in the areas which they inhabit, are absent from the adjoining land areas to the eastward, across which they might be assumed to have journeyed in order to reach the most western island. These plants and animals are not forms which have been evolved within the country. They are known to inhabit other lands ; but these lands, from which the Irish races were derived, lie at a considerable distance to the north or south or west, and are now separated from Ireland by stretches of deep and open sea.

The facts cited above are of such supreme importance

Pipewort (*Eriocaulon septangulare*)

K

that it will be desirable to consider what are some of
the leading animal and plant species which share this
peculiar distribution, where their home is, and how far
they are provided with special means of dispersal which
might admit of the theory that they have crossed the
water into Ireland since the present distribution of land
and sea was established.   The leading species and their
distribution may be summarized as follows :—

MOLLUSKS.   *Helix Pisana.* — IRELAND, east coast.
GREAT BRITAIN, S. Wales and Cornwall. ELSEWHERE,
S. France, Mediterranean, Atlantic Islands.   This is a

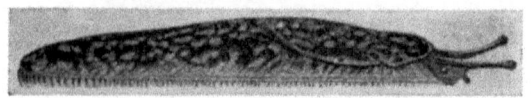

The Kerry Slug (*Geomalacus maculosus*)

pretty little snail inhabiting sand-dunes and other dry
places.

Geomalacus maculosus.—IRELAND, extreme south-
west. GREAT BRITAIN, absent. ELSEWHERE, N.W.
Spain, Portugal.   This is the famous " Spotted Slug "
of Kerry.

BEETLES.   *Pelophila borealis.*—IRELAND, western half.
GREAT BRITAIN, Orkneys.   ELSEWHERE, sub-arctic
Europe.   A little black ground-beetle found on lake
shores.

Otiorrhynchus auropunctatus.—IRELAND, coast from
Wicklow to Donegal. GREAT BRITAIN, unknown.
ELSEWHERE, Pyrenees and Auvergne.   A handsome
species.

SPIDERS. *Tegenaria hibernica*, the Dublin House Spider.—IRELAND, Dublin district mainly, also in the west and south.   Unknown elsewhere, but nearly related to a Pyrenean species.

SHRIMPS. *Mysis relicta.*—IRELAND, a few lakes in the north. GREAT BRITAIN, unknown. ELSEWHERE, Scandinavia, Russia, N. America.   This is a small freshwater shrimp, its relatives being marine.

WOODLICE. This small group furnishes much interesting evidence.   Three species, in Ireland confined to Dublin (*Eluma purpurascens, Metaponorthus melanurus, Philoscia Couchii*), are elsewhere confined to the Mediterranean region and the Atlantic islands, except that the first occurs also in Cornwall.   In addition *Trichoniscus vividus* has the distribution S.E. Ireland, France, Spain ; and *Metapornothus cingendus*, which ranges along the Irish coast from Cork to Mayo and Dublin, is found also in Devon, and, like the last, in France and Spain.

SPONGES. *Heteromeyenia Ryderi*, a sponge which is abundant in lakes in many parts of Ireland and sparingly in western Scotland, is elsewhere known only in N. America.

FLOWERING PLANTS. *Saxifraga umbrosa* and *S. Geum.*—IRELAND, the former widely, the latter more sparingly, along the west coast.   Both found elsewhere only in the Spanish peninsula.   The former is the well-known London Pride.

Arbutus Unedo, the beautiful Strawberry Tree.—IRELAND, Killarney district. GREAT BRITAIN, unknown. ELSEWHERE, from the Bay of Biscay throughout the Mediterranean.

Dabeocia polifolia, Erica mediterranea, E. Mackaii.— These three heaths, characteristic of West Mayo and West Galway, are all confined elsewhere to S.W. France and Spain, the first extending to the Azores. It should be noted that two other heaths, *E. vagans* and *E. ciliaris*, in the British Isles found only in S.W. England, have the same distribution on the Continent.

Pinguicula grandiflora, the lovely Great Butterwort.— IRELAND, south-west. GREAT BRITAIN, unknown. ELSEWHERE, Spanish peninsula and Alps.

Euphorbia hiberna, the Irish Spurge.—IRELAND, along the west coast. GREAT BRITAIN, Devon. ELSE-WHERE, W. France, N. Spain.

Neotinea intacta.—A little Orchid, in Ireland abundant on certain western limestone areas. GREAT BRITAIN, unknown. ELSEWHERE, Mediterranean and Asia Minor.

Spiranthes Romanzoffiana, an interesting and fragrant Orchid.—IRELAND, Lough Neagh basin (N.E.), Kerry, Cork (S.W.). GREAT BRITAIN, unknown. ELSEWHERE, northern N. America, Kamtschatka.

Sisyrinchium angustifolium, the "Blue-eyed grass" of Canada.—IRELAND, widespread in the west. GREAT BRITAIN, unknown. ELSEWHERE, northern N. America.

Simethis bicolor, a slender Liliaceous plant found in Kerry.—GREAT BRITAIN, Dorset. ELSEWHERE, S.W. Europe and the western Mediterranean.

Eriocaulon septangulare, the Pipewort.—IRELAND, west coast. GREAT BRITAIN, Skye. ELSEWHERE, northern N. America.

Glyceria festucæformis, a maritime grass.—IRELAND, Co. Down and Shannon estuary. GREAT BRITAIN, unknown. ELSEWHERE, Mediterranean.

St Dabeoc's Heath (*Dabeocia polifolia*)

The facts of distribution detailed in the case of the foregoing species of animals and plants may be summarized as follows :—quite a number of species which inhabit western Ireland are absent from northern Continental Europe, and have their headquarters in the Spanish Peninsula, in some cases spreading thence eastward along the Mediterranean, or westward and southward to the Atlantic islands. A few species found on the eastern coasts of Ireland, or on both east and west coasts, have a similar distribution. Where any of these occur in Great Britain, as happens in only a few cases, they are confined to south-western England. In addition to this southern group, we find in Ireland a number of remarkable northern forms, elsewhere unknown from such low latitudes, a few of them reappearing in western Scotland. They have their headquarters either in sub-arctic Europe, or in the northern parts of North America.

Now, in endeavouring to arrive at a conclusion as to how these animals and plants of far countries reached Ireland, we have to consider whether they possess special means for rapid or distant dispersal over large areas of sea or land, which would account for their having reached Ireland while other members of the same faunas and floras were left behind. We find that they are not specially favoured in this respect. As regards the animals, it is true that many Beetles have considerable powers of flight, and that Spiders may attain wide dispersal when young by means of gossamer webs. But Mollusks and Woodlice are at all stages of their life-history unprovided with any better means of dispersal than their power of crawling. The Woodlice are particularly sensitive creatures, living half under-

The Mediterranean Orchid *Neotinea intacta* growing among the Alpine-Arctic *Dryas octopetala* in Burren, Co. Clare

ground, many of them unable to endure even a hot sun or a short immersion in water. The Kerry Slug is likewise quite unfitted for adventures by sea or land.

Turning to the plants named above, we find that their powers of dispersal are as a whole low. Plants achieve dispersal almost solely in the seed stage ; many plants possess seeds displaying special characters, such as minute size, lightness, or the presence of parachute appendages, which render possible the performance of daring aerial voyages, or prolonged journeys by water. Other seeds, mostly ones which are embedded in juicy fruits, are eaten by birds, and carried by them over stretches of both land and sea. We find among the plants listed above no preponderance of species possessing such seeds. Two Orchids are indeed in the list, and the seeds of all Orchids are very buoyant in air, owing to the loose netted coat in which they are enclosed ; and one other plant, the Arbutus, has a juicy fruit which is a favourite food of birds. To these we may allow a possibility of fairly distant dispersal, proportionate to the rapid digestion of a bird in the one case, and to the rate of fall of the seeds in the others. In all the other cases, the seeds are devoid of facilities for air-dispersal, and all of them which have been tested (10 out of 13) sink in water—six of them instantly, the remainder after a few days' immersion. It is clear, then, that neither these animals nor plants exhibit as a group modifications which would favour the theory that they migrated direct from their distant homes to the isolated regions which they inhabit in Ireland. It seems more reasonable to look on them as very old inhabitants of the country, which arrived here at distant periods when the distribution of sea and land

London Pride (*Saxifraga umbrosa*)

was different, allowing, in the case of the southern species, of migration along an old western coastline. The problem of the American species is more difficult. But the improbability of direct dispersal is here so great as to suggest a former extension of land, connecting north-western Europe with Greenland and North America by way of Iceland.

This question of the northern and southern elements in the Irish fauna and flora has been dealt with at some length, because it is quite the most interesting problem connected with the natural history of the country. For the rest, the plants and animals occurring in Ireland, and their distribution, accord in general with the position of the island and the physical conditions which prevail upon it. Whatever may be the history of the peculiar northern and southern elements of the fauna and flora there can be no doubt that the bulk of our animals and plants migrated into the country from the eastward, at a time when Ireland formed part of the European mainland, and the difference between Ireland and Great Britain, as regards their animal and vegetable inhabitants, is mainly one of reduction in the further and smaller island. As pointed out on a previous page, the insular position of Ireland and the prevalence of westerly winds combine to render the climate unusually mild, equable, and damp. These features are specially noticeable in the west and south, which are also the regions of greatest exposure. Geological causes such as the nature of the rocks and the discontinuity of the glacial deposits, also combine to render the west and south-west the barest and least cultivated portion of the country. In Donegal, West Mayo, West Galway, Kerry and West Cork in particular, bog, moorland, and rocky mountains occupy large areas.   Woodland is rare, though where shelter is afforded from wind trees grow luxuriantly.   Lakelets are very numerous, lying mostly in rock basins.   Snow and frost are rare, and of short duration.   Cloud and mist are prevalent, and the rainfall is high (40 to 70 inches).   The summers are cool, and drought occurs but seldom.   All of these conditions have their due effect upon life within the area.

In the middle part of Ireland striking changes of surface produce corresponding changes in the nature of the fauna and flora.   Instead of mountains formed of ancient granites, gneisses, slates and sandstones, we have a far-stretching plain of limestone, mostly overlaid by a sheet of limy boulder-clay.   Great peat-bogs occupy much of the surface, with a good deal of wet land and swamp, and small lakes especially towards the west. The River Shannon, meandering southward across the country, spreads out here and there over the plain in broad lake-like expanses.   Rainfall and exposure are less than in the west ; summer is rather warmer, and winter colder.   The effects of these conditions are more fully set out in the more detailed account of the country contained in the other volumes of the series.

In the east we get conditions which conform more nearly to those found in western England.   Lighter soils prevail, and a drier summer than is found elsewhere in Ireland.   Bogland ceases to be a familiar type, and woodland reaches its maximum.   As a result of greater similarity of conditions and of proximity, we find in the east a closer approximation in the fauna and flora to those of Great Britain than is observable elsewhere in Ireland.

As regards the large element in the vegetation which owes its presence to the activities of man, there can be no doubt that the introduction of certain plants—

Rhopalomesites Tardyi and its distribution
in the British Isles

culinary and medicinal herbs in particular—took place at an early period. In medieval times, the monasteries were the centres of dispersal for this section of the flora. Certain species, such as *Inula Helenium, Petroselinum sativum*, etc., are still found associated with the ruins of ancient abbeys ; and certain non-native plants which are now widespread and established, such as *Aegopodium Podagraria, Smyrnium Olusatrum, Allium Babingtonii*, probably owed their first introduction to the monks. The importation of seeds of cereals and of green crops for the use of tillers of the ground has been from early times, as it still is, a fruitful source of alien plants. But as most of these seeds came from the east and south, and belonged to plants accustomed to lighter soils and a warmer climate than are found in Ireland, the bulk of them have not succeeded in establishing themselves ; and those which have done so have their headquarters in eastern Ireland, where climate and soil best suit their requirements. If the list of weed seeds detected in samples of agricultural seeds imported into Ireland be compared with the recorded list of aliens found growing in the country, the high mortality among these immigrants will be apparent. Nevertheless, as elsewhere, introduced plants form a considerable section of the Irish flora, varying in standing from species fully naturalized in the country, and easily holding their own among the native flora, down to fleeting waifs of tilled land, which are present with us only on account of the continual ousting of the native flora by ploughing, and the frequent introduction of fresh seed. The introduction, accidental or deliberate, of new plants still goes on, and occasionally a fresh species obtains a footing in the country, sometimes spreading rapidly. The latest instance of this kind is *Matricaria discoidea*, an American annual first observed in Ireland in 1894, now found on roadsides and waste ground almost all over the country.

Among our animals, introduction does not play nearly so important a part, and is seldom successful unless protection is afforded. The Rabbit, *Lepus cuniculus*, Squirrel, *Sciurus vulgaris*, and Brown Rat, *Mus decumanus*, however, afford instances of successful early introduction—the former two no doubt deliberate, the last accidental. Among the Mollusca, several species, such as *Helix rufescens* and the Testacellas, are considered not indigenous to Ireland ; and among the Beetles, Woodlice, and other groups similar instances occur. But most of the introduced species, such as the Cockroaches and Cricket, only maintain themselves with the aid of the artificial habitat with which man supplies them.

ARCHÆOLOGY, ANTIQUITIES AND ARCHITECTURE

IRELAND is an interesting country in which to pursue archæological studies. In it an unbroken Celtic culture was maintained for an exceptionally long period, remaining almost intact until the sixteenth century A.D. The Roman legions did not penetrate into the island, which escaped the uniform Roman civilisation introduced so largely elsewhere. The Bronze-Age culture of Ireland resembled that of Spain, France and England. These countries forming a Western European group. In early times there seems to have been a lively intercourse between Ireland and the Continent. Irish gold ornaments, approximately dated at 1800 B.C., have been found in Denmark, Germany, France, and Great Britain ; while a large number of amber beads, of prehistoric date, which there is every reason to believe were derived from Scandinavia, have been discovered in Ireland. Certain early types of prehistoric implements indicate Iberian influence. In Roman times Ireland was regarded as lying midway between Spain and Britain, intercourse being then probably carried on between Irish and Spanish ports. The presence of Ogham inscriptions in Ireland as

Typical Flint-flakes from the River Bann

early in date as the fourth century A.D. shows a knowledge of the Latin alphabet previous to the general conversion of the country to Christianity. While a trade in wine between West Gaul and Ireland appears to have existed at least as early as the sixth century A.D.

The majority of Irish archæologists have held the view that man did not inhabit the island during the older Stone Age, known as the Palæolithic period. The reason for this opinion is the presumption that owing to the extension of the northern glaciers, which took place at the end of the Pliocene, and commencement of the Pleistocene period, Ireland was covered with a vast ice cap which rendered human habitation impossible. Recently there has been some reaction against this view ; it has been pointed out that remains of the mammoth have been discovered in various parts of the country ; if the mammoth could exist, it is thought reasonable that man could also have lived.   Further, a large number of the flint implements which have been found on the surface of the soil in the northern counties are similar in type to flints found on the Continent, classified as belonging to the later stages of the Palæolithic culture. But in the absence of stratigraphical evidence it is the safest course to maintain the opinion that Ireland was not inhabited during Palæolithic times.

In the Neolithic period we are on firmer ground. The counties of Antrim and Down are rich in flint, and it is in these localities that nearly all the Irish flint implements have been obtained.   Around the coast of the north-east of Ireland a well-marked shelf or terrace exists ; this terrace or raised beach is one of the geological features which prove that fluctuations of the land and sea level have taken place since the Glacial epoch.   Among these raised beaches that of Larne is the best known.   It is composed of stratified gravel with sandy beds containing numerous specimens of the common univalve shells, flints worked by man being found together with these.   There are similar beaches at the Kinnegar ; Holywood, and Ballyholme Bay, Co. Down ; and at Kilroot ; Carnlough ; etc., in Antrim. At Greenore in Co. Louth and other spots round the north-eastern coast, similar deposits of elevated marine

gravels and sands may be observed.   As well as flakes,
flint cores and implements of a typical character are
found at Larne, the importance of the site being due to

Neolithic Stone Axe-heads from the North of Ireland

the fact that the worked flints found in it have been
considered to be the earliest proofs of man's habitation
of this island.   Recently the similarity between the
type of chipped celt found at Larne and those discovered
at Cissbury, near Worthing, Sussex, has been insisted

L

upon. The Cissbury finds have been claimed as belonging to the late Palæolithic period, but their date is at present the subject of controversy. The likeness between the implements from Larne and those from Cissbury is striking, and, if the Cissbury remains are finally established as Palæolithic in date, our ideas as to the date of the Larne implements may undergo some alteration.

The sandhills of the north coast of Ireland have yielded several occupation sites of Neolithic man. The principal are at Dundrum Bay, Co. Down ; Whitepark Bay, Co. Antrim ; and the mouth of the river Bann, near Portstewart, Co. Londonderry. These sandhills overlie the raised beach, and in old surfaces laid bare by the wind numerous worked flints and pieces of pottery are found. The industry of these sites is of a more advanced character than that of Larne ; they seem to have been occupied through the Neolithic, Bronze, Early Iron, and Christian periods.

Large numbers of flint scrapers, arrow-heads, javelin-heads, knives, etc., have been found in Ireland ; the workmanship of many of these is remarkable. The ordinary polished celts of Neolithic times have been found in all parts of the Island.

Little pottery belonging to the Neolithic period has been recovered ; but from the extant remains it appears to have consisted of small vessels with rounded bases, which later developed into the typical " food-vessels " of the Bronze Age.

Dolmens (dolmen=*dol*, a table and *men*, a stone), may be roughly classified as belonging to the Neolithic period, though a few may be as late as the Bronze Age. The types vary in the different counties as will be noticed, but the normal dolmen is constructed of a number of large rough slabs set on end with a larger covering slab on the top. It has been computed that there are 780 dolmens in Ireland distributed as follows :— 248 in Connaught, 234 in Munster, 227 in Ulster and 71 in Leinster. Numerous theories have been advanced as to

Proleek Cromlech, Co. Louth

the use of dolmens. Excavations made in the floors of many examples have, however, revealed human remains, and it is now generally admitted that they were places of burial. They are widely distributed throughout the world, being found in India, Syria, the Caucasus, different parts of the northern coast of the Black Sea, North Africa, Spain, Portugal, France, Belgium, Holland, North Germany, Denmark, Sweden, and the British

Islands. Dolmens are also common in Japan, but they belong to a later period, being of Iron - Age date.

Stone circles are numerous in Ireland; their use appears to have been partly ceremonial and partly sepulchral. Pillar stones are also frequently to be seen. One, a monolith of granite, situated close to Punchestown Racecourse, Co. Kildare, is 19½ ft. in height. The worship of stones was common in many countries in ancient times. The Irish pillar stones may probably be regarded as connected with the cult of the dead.

The first metal used for making implements and weapons in Ireland was copper, which is plentiful in the island. The principal deposits form three groups near the coast, situated in the counties of Wicklow, Waterford, Cork, and Kerry. A large amount of copper was raised from the Irish mines in the last century, 1157 tons of copper were exported from Ireland and sold at Swansea in the year 1855. Ancient stone implements have been discovered in Co. Waterford in old copper workings showing that it was mined in early times. The discovery and utilisation of copper did not displace the use of stone implements, which continued in service side by side with those of metal. Large stone celts must have been more formidable than many of the small and weak copper axes that have been found. The time during which copper was in use was a comparatively short one. A large number of copper celts have been found in various parts of Ireland; some of the scythe-shaped blades, known as halberts, are also made of copper; they are probably contemporary with the copper celts. This transitional copper period

Pillar Stone, Punchestown, Co. Kildare

probably ended about 1800 B.C., after which the true
Bronze Age commenced.

The Irish Bronze Age is characterised by the extraordinary skill displayed in casting some of the more
advanced types of weapons such as rapiers, dagger-
blades, and spear-heads. Bronze is a mixture of copper
and tin, the usual proportion being one part of tin to
nine of copper. The amount of native tin in Ireland is
too small to have supplied sufficient metal for alloying
the copper used for making bronze implements, so it must
have been imported, but whence it is impossible to say
for certain. Possibly it may have come from Spain at
first, and later from Britain. The earlier implements
are flat bronze axe-heads, and short, weak knife-daggers.
These were replaced later by socketed axe-heads, long
daggers, rapiers, leaf-shaped swords, and elaborate
spear-heads of different forms. Bronze razors, sickles,
and a large series of trumpets of late Bronze-Age date
have also been found. Some of the latter are truly
remarkable specimens of the art of bronze casting.
The Irish gold deposits were worked during the same
period, and Ireland's great wealth in this precious metal
must have made her the richest country in Western
Europe. There are over five hundred objects of gold,
all of which have been found in Ireland, preserved in
the Royal Irish Academy's collection in the National
Museum, Dublin : the major portion of these belong to
the Bronze Age. There are many references to gold
ornaments and payments of gold by weight in the
ancient literature of Ireland ; the Book of Leinster, a
MS. of the twelfth century, refers the first smelting of
gold to the forests east of the River Liffey, the present
Wicklow gold district. As late as the eighteenth century

gold was discovered in Ballinvally stream at Croghan Kinshelagh, Co. Wicklow.   The Government undertook mining operations there, and gold to the amount of 945 ounces was collected in some two years.

The Irish Bronze Age probably continued until about 400 B.C. when it was replaced by the second Iron Age or La Tène culture.

Only two finds of the so-called "drinking cups," or beakers (a type of vessel common in England and on the Continent, belonging to the earliest phase of the Bronze Age) have been discovered in Ireland; they consisted of the remains of three vessels found together at Moytura, Co. Sligo; and of a beaker, stated to have been found at Mount Stewart, Co. Down, the latter vessel has been unfortunately destroyed, and the particulars as to its discovery are uncertain.   The vessels of this period most frequently discovered belong to the so-called "food-vessel" class; they were developed

Gold Lunula and Collar, National Museum, Dublin

from the round-bottomed urn of Neolithic times, their evolution being easily traceable when a number of examples of different types are placed together. Food vessels are often richly ornamented ; they continued in use during the greater part of the Bronze Age, being found with both burnt and unburnt interments ; in many cases they contained, when found, cremated bones. In the later portion of the Bronze Age, large vessels, termed cinerary urns, are common. They have been frequently found in an inverted position containing cremated bones ; small vessels called " pigmy-cups " are often found associated in interments with cinerary urns.

The ethnology of Ireland is a difficult problem. The name " Late Celtic," which is sometimes applied to Irish objects of Iron Age date decorated with La Tène ornament, causes an idea that the Bronze-Age population of Ireland were Celts. But iron weapons being the distinguishing mark of the Celt, it is probable that this people did not reach Ireland much before the fourth century B.C., and that they then came directly from the Continent rather than across England. The racial affinities of the earlier population must for the present remain uncertain. The Bronze-Age people may have belonged to a western branch of the so-called Mediterranean race. The Hallstatt period (first Continental Iron Age) is not at present well represented among Irish finds, but a variety of Continental Iron-Age types such as swords, trumpets, round shields, buckets, and caldrons have been discovered in Ireland : these antiquities no doubt found their way to the island under Hallstatt influence. The true La Tène period probably commenced in Ireland only about 400 B.C. The derivation of the characteristic La Tène ornament, with its swelling curves and trumpet-shaped ends, from the classical palmette, has been so often described that there is no need to discuss it here. Among the principal objects surviving from this period are bridle-bits, and head ornaments for horses; finely decorated sword sheaths from Lisnacroghera crannog; some bronze discs; and a few brooches of a very beautiful pattern. Few iron weapons belonging to this period have been preserved, but among them are swords, and some spear-heads; one of the latter is set with enamel, while another has its socket ornamented with settings of gold. That the La Tène style had taken a deep root in Ireland previous to the introduction of Christianity is shown by three stone monuments decorated with La Tène ornament which have been found in different parts of Ireland, one at Turoe, Co. Galway; another at Castlestrange, Co. Roscommon; and the third, which is later in date probably belonging to the Christian period, in Co. Kildare. The size of these monuments makes it certain that they were carved in the island, not imported.

Sword-sheaths from
Lisnacroghera
Crannog

Christianity was probably first introduced into Ireland by Gaulish traders, but the general conversion of the island did not take place until the coming of St Patrick in the fifth century. In the early portion of the Christian period the pagan La Tène ornament survived, the decoration being confined to survivals from the La Tène period In the seventh and eighth centuries a new style of ornament was introduced known from its prevailing patterns as the "Interlaced style." Interlaced patterns were probably originally derived from Roman plait-work, which is common on mosaic pavements, but, in the case of Ireland it may be suggested that such patterns were not directly derived from Roman sources, but were introduced as part of the general scheme of Christian ornament, which was influenced by Syria and Egypt. St Patrick, it may be recalled, had been educated at the semi-oriental monastery of Lérins. These interlaced patterns developed into beautiful and intricate forms: combined with zoomorphic (animal) ornament, and many varieties of fret patterns, they became eventually the most characteristic feature of Irish ornament.

The derivation of Irish zoomorphic ornament is complicated. Frequently it has been ascribed to a Germanic source on account of the similarities to be observed between the characteristic German and Scandinavian ornament and that of Ireland. It is however probable that the similarity may be ultimately traced to a common origin *i.e.* the Nearer East, rather than to any direct reciprocal influence between Ireland and the Germanic lands.

The Irish monasteries and monastic schools, such as

Bangor, Co. Down ; Clonmacnois, King's Co., and many others, enjoyed during this period a deservedly high reputation both as centres of learning and schools of art. The illuminated MSS. produced by the Irish monastic scribes are admitted to be among the finest in the whole decorated series. The most celebrated Irish illuminated MS. is the Book of Kells preserved in the library of Trinity College, Dublin: it is probably of early eighth century date. The earlier illuminated MSS. display spiral ornaments derived from the preceding pagan period, while in the later examples the decoration consists principally of interlaced work. Mr O. M. Dalton (*Byzantine Art and Archæology*, 1911), has pointed out that the seated figures of the Evangelists writing, which occur in the Irish MSS., can only have been derived from East-Christian illuminated gospels of the sixth century, for the types were unknown elsewhere. The scenes which include human figures, however fantastic they may appear, are probably only distorted versions of compositions first popularised in the Christian East. The figure subjects on the High Crosses of tenth century and later date are due to similar influence. The representations of Christ in Glory so frequently carved on the High Crosses, where the Saviour is represented with a sceptre over one shoulder and a cross over the other are suggestive of Egyptian influence.

The two most celebrated pieces of Irish metal-work extant, the Tara Brooch and the Ardagh Chalice, belong to this period. The Tara Brooch was found in 1850 on the strand at Bettystown, near Drogheda. It has no connection with Tara, but was named the " Tara Brooch " by the jeweller to whom it was sold. The body of the brooch is bronze ; it is decorated with panels in

fine gold filigree work, enamel, and settings of amber
and of glass. The various forms of ornamentation
comprise spirals, interlaced, and zoomorphic decoration,
and human heads. The ornament on the front consists

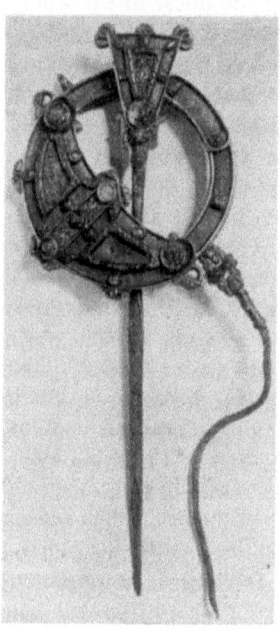

mostly of interlaced work ;
on the back spiral designs
are more prominent. A
special feature of the ornament are the minute beadings
placed on the upper edge of
the ribbons, out of which
some of the interlaced
patterns are formed. The
ornamentation of the brooch
shows many analogies with
the patterns of the Books
of Kells, and of Durrow ;
it may be assigned to the
eighth century A.D.

The Ardagh Chalice was
found in 1868 with a small
cup-shaped vessel of bronze
and four brooches, in the
rath of Reerastra, near
the village of Ardagh, Co.
Limerick. This chalice, the
only example of a Celtic

The Tara Brooch

chalice that has been preserved, is one of the finest and
most beautifully balanced works of art in the world.
It is composed of no less than 354 different pieces : the
enamels with which it is decorated are marvellously fine.
Probably it is slightly later in date than the Tara Brooch.

Many other beautiful examples of Irish workmanship

of the Christian period, including the Cross of Cong (about 1123 A.D.), can be studied in the National Museum in Dublin.

The Vikings who commenced to plunder Ireland in the eighth century, established in the ninth century settlements in various parts of the country.   An in-

The Ardagh Chalice

teresting series of finds derived from the Scandinavian settlements in Ireland is preserved in the National Collection, Dublin.   The objects include the characteristic iron swords, brooches, scales and weights. etc., the majority having been obtained from a Norse cemetery at Kilmainham, Dublin.   The Norsemen in their earlier raids committed terrible destruction, and there can be little doubt that many of the treasures of the Irish monasteries were by them destroyed.   Afterwards they became converted to Christianity and settled down peacefully with the Irish, a mixed style of art being then produced known as the "Hiberno-Danish Style," of which the

The Cross of Cong

Bell-Shrine of St Patrick (about 1100 A.D.) is an example. This Hiberno-Danish style appears to have been brought to an end after the Anglo-Norman invasion when it was replaced by the general Romanesque and Gothic styles.

Ogham inscriptions are not confined to Ireland; they occur in the Isle of Man, Scotland, Wales and the south-west of England, but of a total number of about 360 known inscriptions more than five-sixths have been found in Ireland. The Irish inscriptions number some 300; of these five-sixths have been found in the counties of Kerry, Cork, and Waterford. Co. Kerry contains about 120 inscriptions, Co. Cork about 80, and Waterford about 40. A few inscriptions have been found in East Meath and Ossory, but throughout the remainder of Ireland they are exceptional. The Ogham alphabet consists of four groups of strokes arranged in reference to a single base line, usually the edge of the stone upon which they are engraved. The vowels are represented by small notches upon the stave line, other letters by strokes either to the left or right of the line, or crossing it obliquely. The script is based upon the Latin alphabet. The bulk of the inscriptions may be ascribed to the fifth and sixth centuries A.D., some appear to be as early as the fourth century, these are of interest as showing a knowledge of the Latin alphabet in Ireland previous to the general conversion of the island to Christianity in the fifth century. Ogham inscriptions are of a commemorative character, usually consisting of the name of an individual and that of his father.

Lake dwellings, or, as they are usually called, crannogs, are numerous in Ireland. They generally consist of small islets of clay or marl in a lake, which were enlarged and surrounded by timber, the floor being formed of branches of trees; in some cases they were strengthened by stones. It is possible that the occupation of some lake dwellings may go back to the prehistoric period, but the finds are extremely mixed, and crannogs appear to have been used as retreats until very late times. One was taken by storm by the English in the reign of Queen Elizabeth. The *Irish Annals* contain many references to crannogs from the ninth to the seventeenth centuries A.D.

Probably the most beautiful objects as yet recovered from an Irish crannog are the three bronze sword sheaths decorated with La Tène ornament discovered in the crannog of Lisnacroghera, Co. Antrim.

The ordnance maps mark some 28,800 forts of various kinds in Ireland, 4,283 being in Ulster, 4,651 in Leinster, 7,593 in Connaught and 12,232 in Munster. These figures are probably much below the actual number of forts in the country. Whether the forts are built of earth or stone depends largely on the nature of the country. Where stone and earth are plentiful, forts are built of both materials. Where stone is abundant earth forts are rare. For the purposes of this introduction Irish forts may be divided roughly into the following :—

1. *Promontory Forts.* This type includes cliff forts, in which the sea forms a natural defence on one side ; and inland forts built on the spurs of hill sides. The fortification may consist of a wall, with or without a fosse, or of several earthworks and fosses. The walls usually show a convex curve to the landside. There are numerous promontory forts in Ireland such as those of Dunmore, and Dunbeg, Corcaguiney, Co. Kerry. The fort of Caherconree in the same county is a specimen of the inland type built on the spur of a hill. There are some interesting examples of cliff forts along the

eastern coast of Waterford. Promontory forts are generally considered to be early in date ; some no doubt go back as far as the Bronze Age ; but their age is difficult to estimate, as many appear to have been rebuilt and occupied at very different periods.

2. *Ring Forts*. This, the most common type of fort, includes numberless varieties, both of size and structural material. In its simplest form the ring fort is merely a piece of land encircled by a wall of earth or stone, of varying height, with a fosse outside the ring. More elaborate examples have several walls or earth-works and fosses up to the number of seven rings. The earthen forts outnumber those built of stone ; the latter are often remarkable monuments with immensely strong walls and remains of hut sites, or dwellings, inside them. Both earth and stone forts frequently contain under-ground passages called *souterrains*, which were probably used for storing grain and food stuffs, and also, possibly, as a last refuge should the fort be stormed by the enemy. Passages of this kind have often been explored, but have yielded few objects ; these as a rule belong to late periods and are insufficient to determine the date of *souterrains*. Ring forts, both those made of stone and those of earth, must vary greatly in date ; some, like the Longstone Rath at Furness, near Naas, Co. Kildare, which contained a Bronze-Age burial, are of early date, but many of the smaller rings are probably the remains of mediæval homesteads, recalling the time when it was usual to surround dwellings with a wall and fosse. Others may have been mere cattle pens. The great stone forts such as those at Aran are difficult to date, but archæologists of repute consider that they may be placed in the Bronze Age.

M

3. *Rectangular Forts.* In these the walls are straight, and except for their plan they are identical with the ring forts. This type occurs in most of the Irish counties, but is especially numerous in south Leinster. Taken as a whole these forts appear to be the latest of the various types ; some may belong to the period of the Anglo-Norman invasion of Ireland.

4. *Motes.* A mote is a mound of earth generally about 20 ft. to 40 ft. high with steep sides, and a flat top from about 30 ft. to 100 ft. across : the mound as a rule is circular in plan, and may be wholly or partly artificial, with, frequently, an attached fortified court or bailey. The mote is usually surrounded by a fosse as is also the bailey, the ditch of the latter usually joining that of the mound. The bailey is often shield- or crescent-shaped ; it is frequently hard to trace the remains of either bailey or fosse, which causes confusion between earthworks that are undoubtedly Norman motes and others that are just as certainly Celtic tumuli. The Normans probably made use of any suitable mound for the purpose of a mote-castle, thus many so-called Norman motes may only be re-used Celtic tumuli. Motes represent the earliest military buildings of the Normans in Ireland, the flat top was doubtless surmounted by a battlemented tower of wood with a palisade round its upper edge, with a similar defence upon the earthen ramparts below, and also upon the wall surrounding the bailey. The tower on the top of the mote was connected with the bailey by a bridge. The numerous references to the burning of castles during the Anglo-Norman conquest refer to these early wooden buildings. In later times the wooden tower was replaced by a stone keep, while the walls were also constructed of

stones. Motes are common in the counties occupied by the Normans; becoming less numerous outside the early Norman settlements. They are found at the chief manorial seats in the Anglo-Norman lordships of Meath, Leinster, and Ulster. There are few in Connaught.

ARCHITECTURE

The most remarkable monuments of architecture belonging to the prehistoric period are the chambered burial tumuli, of which Newgrange and Dowth are the best known examples. In these the roof is constructed by over-sailing slabs which narrow so as to form what may be called a false dome or a false vault, while the passages and chambers are built of large undressed stones set on end. The dry-built stone forts such as the Staigue fort in Kerry with its remarkable stairways, and the great fort at Aran with abattis and doorways are also instances of the skill of the prehistoric architects.

A striking feature of the early Christian architecture of Ireland are the small stone oratories of the seventh century. These small oratories or churches were built without mortar, having roofs of the beehive type. They are quite small and rectangular in shape measuring generally fifteen feet in length, and ten in breadth. The wooden oratory of the same type was called a *Dairthech* (oak-house). None of these have survived. The stone oratories are without any external or internal decoration save for an occasional example, which has a cross of white stones built in above the doorway. The well-known oratory of Gallerus on the Dingle peninsula, Co. Kerry, is a typical example; rectangular in plan, it is roofed by a species of false

doming.   From these dry-stone oratories were developed
the stone-roofed churches built with mortar, such as those
of the monastic settlement at Glendalough, Co. Wicklow.

Donaghmore Round Tower, Navan

Ireland contains numerous examples of churches of
this early type in a more or less ruined condition.

A word may be said about the "round towers" which,
though not peculiar to Ireland, are often considered to
be the most characteristic buildings in the island.   The

towers, which are generally about twenty feet in external diameter, vary from sixty to one hundred and ten feet in height. They are always found in connexion with the early ecclesiastical settlements in Ireland, and may be dated from the end of the ninth to the following two centuries. Several essays have been written with a view to establishing a pagan origin for these towers, they are, however, undoubtedly Christian, and, as stated above, are late in date, being nothing but detached belfries, which were useful as storehouses ; they also probably served as places of retreat for the ecclesiastics during the Viking raids.

The noblest remaining example of Irish Romanesque architecture is the group of buildings on the rock of Cashel, Co. Tipperary, which can be dated to the middle of the twelfth century. Other remarkable examples of about the same date are to be seen at Freshford, Co. Kilkenny ; Tuam ; Clonfert ; and the Nuns Church at Clonmacnois, King's Co. Irish Romanesque architecture presents many problems, the principal of which is to what extent it is derived directly from the Continent. There can be little doubt that many of the ornamental details were based upon classical models indirectly derived through Syria and Ravenna.

After the Anglo-Norman invasion Irish Romanesque architecture was replaced by Gothic. The Transitional period from the Romanesque to the Gothic style can be studied in some of the Cistercian abbeys built about A.D. 1200 such as Boyle Abbey, Co. Roscommon ; Abbey Knockmoy, Co. Galway; and Corcomroe, Co. Clare. There are some good Irish examples of thirteenth-century buildings in the so-called Early-English style as also of the later periods ;

but the Gothic architecture of Ireland is no mere slavish
copy of English models ; it exhibits peculiarities of
great interest, and it seems doubtful if English influence

Corcomroe Abbey, Co. Clare

played such a preponderating part in its development
as sometimes is thought.

There are some 118 decorated High Crosses in Ireland,
there being roughly 32 in Ulster, 25 in Munster, 8 in
Connaught, and 53 in Leinster.   The free standing wheel
cross is known from the beginning of the tenth century
A.D. : one of the crosses that can be dated by its inscription, the cross of Muiredach at Monasterboice,

belongs to the year A.D. 924. The origin of the wheel cross is probably to be sought in the combination of the wheel, the well-known sun symbol, with the Christian

High Cross, Clonmacnois, King's Co.

cross. The evolution from a plain cross with a disc surrounded by a circle in the centre can be traced on Irish examples. The High Crosses are among the most interesting monuments in Ireland. Usually they are carved with a representation of the Crucifixion on one side of the head, and Our Lord in glory on the other, the uprights being divided into panels, carved with various scenes from the Old and New Testament. In some cases, as at Ahenny, Co. Tipperary, the ornamentation is confined to geometrical and interlaced designs. The interlaced and spiral patterns carved on the crosses are combined and executed in a manner that is beyond praise, the figure sculpture is, however, apt to strike observers as barbarous. But it should be remembered that the artistic genius of the Celts did not lie in the direction of figure drawing, also that the figures are only pale reflections of Byzantine models, the latter being themselves based upon Hellenistic art. It is also to be borne in mind that the Byzantine art from which the Irish sculptors derived their inspiration was Hieratic, the different scenes being represented in a traditional manner that left the artist little scope for original treatment. On the bases of the High Crosses, where are portrayed non-religious scenes, the figures have a more life-like appearance. The iconography of the High Crosses cannot here be discussed: it is a large subject upon which much has been written, though no comprehensive study has been produced.

ADMINISTRATION

FROM the time when, in the reign of Henry II, Strongbow, acting in defiance of the king, intervened in a tribal quarrel, Ireland has in a greater or lesser degree been subservient to England. The English power at this period dominated the districts of Drogheda, Dublin, Wexford, Waterford, and Cork, an area which constituted what was known as the " English Pale." The English barons of the Pale never overcame the tribes beyond its border, and were at feud with each other and disaffected towards the English Government. These tribes were, moreover, so divided by feuds and quarrels that they were powerless to expel the invaders. The English domination became more effective under Henry the Eighth, and the power of the Crown was acknowledged throughout the country.

The parliamentary history of the English Colony in Ireland follows closely that of England. The Irish Parliament was indeed a counterpart of the British Parliament. It had its hereditary House of Peers and the laws regulating the parliamentary franchise were, before the Union with Great Britain, exactly the same in both countries. At first there were informal meetings of important persons. In 1295 there was a parliament of which some Acts remain. To this only Knights of the Shire were summoned to represent the Commons. Burgesses were added in 1310. There are records of the Parliament of 1374 to which twenty members were summoned to the House of Commons from the counties of Dublin, Louth, Kildare, and

Carlow, the liberties and " Crosses " of Meath, the city of Dublin, and the towns of Drogheda and Dundalk. Writs were addressed for another parliament in the same year to a much larger number of counties and towns. The number of representatives does not appear to have much exceeded 60, but in 1613 James I, by a wholesale creation of new boroughs, increased the House of Commons to 232.

Originally the " lord deputy " (the first Lord-Lieutenant was appointed as early as 1173) appears to have held parliaments at his option, and their Acts were the only statutory law which applied to Ireland. In 1495, however, the Irish Parliament passed an Act known as Poynings' Law (after the lord deputy of the time) or the Statute of Drogheda. This enacted that all the laws of England antecedent to that date were deemed good and effectual in Ireland. It was further secured that initiative of legislation should rest with the English Privy Council. The procedure came to be as follows : Propositions for laws might originate in either of the Irish Houses. After two readings and a committal they were sent by the Irish Privy Council to England. They were afterwards returned to the Irish Council and submitted to the House in which they had originated ; after passing three readings (and, in the case of bills originating in the Commons, passing through the same stages in the House of Lords) they received the royal assent from the Lord-Lieutenant. Any bill was liable to rejection or amendment in all these stages, but when they had passed the Great Seal of England no alteration could be made by the Irish Parliament. This was regarded as a misinterpretation of Poynings' Law and obviously entailed a serious encroachment upon the constitution as it had previously existed in Ireland. The freedom of the Irish Parliament to legislate for Ireland had been vitally and adversely affected.

The state of things described in the preceding paragraph was profoundly modified by legislation in 1782. As a result of this it was necessary that bills passed by the Irish Parliament should be sent to England to receive the Great Seal after which they required the royal assent. From this date until 1800 the Irish Government consisted of the Lord-Lieutenant and his Chief Secretary by whom he was represented in the Irish House of Commons. These were chosen by the English Government and went in and out of office with that Government. Thus the Irish Administration was responsible to the English Government, and was virtually independent of the Irish Parliament.

In 1801 the Irish Parliament ceased to exist and Ireland became legislatively united with Great Britain by the Act of Union. The representation of Ireland in the new Parliament of the United Kingdom was fixed, and the subjects of the two countries given equal rights. The majority of the Irish people have never ceased, however, to demand, through their representatives in parliament, a measure of " Home Rule " for Ireland.

We are now in a position to deal with the Irish Administration of to-day. The Irish Government consists of the Lord-Lieutenant or Viceroy, who is the representative of the Crown and the head of the Executive. Either he or his Chief Secretary, but usually the latter, is in the Cabinet, and both go out of office with the Government. The Lord-Lieutenant is assisted by a Privy Council. In the absence of the Lord-Lieutenant his functions are discharged by Lord Justices sworn for the purpose. Each county is in charge of a Lieutenant and Deputy-Lieutenants. The seat of Government in Ireland is Dublin Castle, but there is in Old Queen Street, London, an " Irish Office "

Sackville Street, Dublin

which, especially during the sessions of Parliament, is kept in close touch with Dublin Castle. In Dublin Castle are the headquarters of the Chief Secretary and Under-Secretary or Under-Secretaries, the Law Officers of the Crown, the Lord Chancellor, the Inspector-General and Deputy-Inspector-General of the Royal Irish Constabulary and other important officials. The Chief Secretary is not only the parliamentary head of the whole Irish Administration, but also the head of every department of it.

The executive functions of Irish Government are carried out by a number of Boards, Commissions, and a Department of State. The more important of these are the following :

Local Government Board.
Department of Agriculture and Technical Instruction.
Congested Districts Board.
Land Commission.
Estates Commission.
Office of Public Works.
Board of National Education.
Intermediate Education Board.

Local Government Board.—This Board consists of the Chief Secretary as President, a Vice-President, the Under Secretary, and two Commissioners. It was established in 1872 and there were transferred to it certain functions previously performed by the Lord-Lieutenant, the Privy Council, and the Chief Secretary in reference to Local Government. It is now the central authority for Poor Law, Local Government, and Public Health matters. An important reform was established in 1898 when the Local Government (Ireland) Act was placed on the Statute Book. Functions which had been performed by the grand juries were transferred to County Councils then for the first time created. The local authorities are now the County Councils, Municipal Corporations, Urban and Rural District Councils.

The Department of Agriculture and Technical Instruction was established by Act in 1899, and was endowed with wide powers and responsibilities in connection with agricultural development and technical education. It was also entrusted with duties in relation to Irish fisheries and to veterinary work. Certain large public institutions were transferred to its control among which are the Royal College of Science, the National Museum, National Library, National Gallery, Metropolitan School of Art, and the Albert Agricultural College at Glasnevin. The Chief Secretary is the President, and there is a Vice-President, Secretary and Assistant Secretaries for Agriculture and Technical Instruction.

The Congested Districts Board was called into existence in 1891, and embodied an attempt on the part of the State to ameliorate the conditions of life of the inhabitants of the poorest districts of the western coast. It was declared (Purchase of Land (Ireland) Act 1891) that when more than 20 per cent. of the population of any county in Ireland live in electoral divisions of which the total rateable value, when divided by the number of the population, gives a sum of less than thirty shillings for each individual, such electoral divisions shall be deemed to form a separate county known as a Congested Districts County. The districts thus declared "congested" embraced part of each county in Connaught and part of Clare, Cork, Kerry, and Donegal. The population in these districts are thus seen to be "congested" not as regards "density" but as regards the sufficiency of land for its support. The Board was empowered to direct its efforts to the improvement of agriculture by increasing the size of small-holdings, by the improvement of live stock, methods of cultivation, and by the development of suitable industries such as fishing, weaving, spinning, etc. By an Act of 1909 the area of the congested

Land re-settled by the Congested Districts Board

districts was more than doubled, and the functions
of the Board were modified in certain respects. A

(*Above*) **Old Type of Cottage in the West of Ireland**

(*Below*) **Type of Labourers' Cottage with which the Congested Districts Board is replacing the old insanitary cabins**

large amount of work has been done towards the
amelioration of the conditions of life in these poor

districts, and many areas have been "striped," new cottages built and the peasants resettled.

The Irish Land Commission was brought into being to administer the legislation enacted with a view to remedying the evils of the Irish Land question. The Acts date from 1870, and empower the Commission to fix fair rents, and to advance moneys to enable tenants to purchase their holdings.

The Commission comprises two Judicial Commissioners and three others.

Up to 1918 the number of rents fixed for a *first statutory term* of 15 years was 382,642, the average reduction in the rents being about 20 per cent. Large numbers of these have been fixed for second and third terms, reduction of rents being effected in each case.

Nearly twenty-four millions sterling have been advanced under the Acts passed up to 1896, the area involved being 2,456,031 acres. The money advanced is being repaid to the State over a term of years by annual payments. These payments are considerably less than the former rental.

The Estates Commission consists of three of the five Land Commissioners. It was created by the Land Act of 1903 in order to speed up the purchasing of land. The system was revolutionised, whole estates were purchased and not merely holdings as under previous Acts. The buyer's annuity was reduced from 4 per cent. to $3\frac{1}{4}$ per cent. of the purchase money. The Commission was also empowered to buy and redistribute land with the object of relieving congestion, and to improve the condition of the estates sold. It was given charge also of the reinstatement of evicted tenants. The Commission works in close co-operation with the Congested Districts Board.

N

Another Act was passed in 1909, and under the two Acts over sixty-nine millions have been advanced in respect of holdings already vested in purchasing tenants, the area involved being 6,530,237 acres. This latter figure, together with the area covered by the previous Acts makes a total of nearly half the area of the island.

Office of Public Works.—The Commissioners of Public Works in Ireland are responsible for the provision and maintenance of the buildings utilised as State and official residences in Ireland, for the provision of accommodation for the civil and legal Government Departments, and for certain works in connection with Coast Guard Buildings, the Royal Hospital at Kilmainham, the Royal Hibernian Military School, the Metropolitan Police and Royal Irish Constabulary quarters, etc. The Commissioners are also charged with the upkeep of the royal harbours of Kingstown, Howth, Donaghadee, Dunmore, and Ardglass, and with the maintenance in efficient repair of the works constructed under the Marine Works Act of 1902.

Phœnix Park, St Stephen's Green Park, Dublin, and the Curragh of Kildare are in charge of the Board, as is also the preservation of the vast majority of the important national and ancient ruins and monuments throughout the country.

The Board are empowered under various Acts of Parliament to make loans for various public works such as country roads, bridges, and courthouses; harbours, docks, and canals; fishery piers; navigation works; public libraries, reformatories, and schools; sanitary improvements including water supply and sewerage; housing of the working classes; arterial drainage; reclamation of waste lands and land improvement;

farm buildings, etc. The total of all loan advances
made up to the 31st March 1919, was £51,766,330.

In addition to the above there has recently been
established an Irish Public Health Council under the
office of the Minister of Health for Ireland who is the
Chief Secretary.

The Custom-House, Dublin
(Before its destruction by fire in May 1921)

There have also been established during the last few
years branches of the following United Kingdom Services.
The Board of Trade exercise certain functions in Ireland,
and the Ministries of Labour and of Transport also have
branches in Ireland.   There are also Customs and Excise,
Inland Revenue and the Post Office, the Irish Commission
of National Health Insurance, the Ordnance Survey, etc.

The functions of the Board of National Education (dealing with primary education) and the Intermediate Education Board (dealing with secondary education) are dealt with under the heading of " Education."

Legal Administration.—The Lord Chancellor of Ireland is head of the Irish judicial establishment. The House of Lords is the final Court of Appeal from the Irish Courts as well as from those of Great Britain. There is a Supreme Court divided into a Court of Appeal and a High Court of Justice, the latter being subdivided into the Chancery Division (including the Landed Estates Court) and the King's Bench Division (including the Courts for Probate and Matrimonial Causes, etc.). The County Courts have limited jurisdiction in matters of contract, etc. with an appeal in equity to the Chancery Division or to a Judge of Assize, and in Common Law to a Judge of Assize. There are Criminal Courts, viz. the Court of Crown Cases Reserved and the Assize Courts similar to those in England. The Courts of Quarter Sessions are presided over by a County Court judge. Minor offences are dealt with by Courts of Summary Jurisdiction and Petty Sessions.

Royal Irish Constabulary.[1]—This semi-military force consisted of about 10,000 members. These lived in barracks and were drilled as soldiers. They have in the past performed many duties not required from other police forces, such as collecting agricultural statistics, acting as inspectors of weights and measures, and as inspectors under the Food and Drugs Act.

The City of Dublin has a special police force—the Dublin Metropolitan Police under a Chief Commissioner whose offices are in Dublin Castle.

[1] This force is now disbanded, and a Civic Guard is being organised under the direction of the Provisional Government.

THE GOVERNMENT OF IRELAND ACT, 1920

Considerable changes in the administrative system as outlined above were involved in the Act which was placed on the Statute Book towards the close of 1920. The Act set up a parliament for Northern Ireland which would include the counties of Antrim, Armagh, Down, Fermanagh, Londonderry, and Tyrone, and the cities of Belfast and Londonderry, and a government for Southern Ireland (*i.e.* the rest of Ireland). The Act contemplated ultimate union between the two governments, and with a view to the establishment of a single parliament for all Ireland there was to be created a *Council of Ireland*, consisting of twenty representatives elected by each parliament, and a President, nominated by the Lord-Lieutenant. With a view to securing uniform administration, certain services were placed under the jurisdiction of the Council, viz. railways, fisheries, and contagious diseases of animals. The two parliaments might, if they agreed, transfer to the Council any other matters affecting the whole country and which might properly be administered by the Council. Certain matters of Imperial concern were excluded from the power of the northern and southern parliaments and governments such as the making of peace and war, foreign relations, naval, military, and air force matters. Matters affecting external trade and commerce, marine navigation, merchant shipping, etc., Customs and Excise were also excluded. The postal service, post office and trustee savings banks, designs for stamps, the registration of deeds and the Public Record Office of Ireland were temporarily reserved to the United Kingdom Parliament and Government to which Land Purchase was also reserved.

As to the Judicature, the Supreme Court for the whole of Ireland was abolished and there was to be a Supreme Court for southern Ireland, a Supreme Court for northern Ireland and a High Court of Appeal for all Ireland to which appeals would lie from each of the new Supreme Courts. Decisions of the new High Court of Appeal for Ireland would be subject to an appeal to the House of Lords. The office of Lord Chancellor of Ireland was to cease to be a political or executive office, and the Lord Chancellor was to be President of the High Court of Appeal for Ireland.

While the Act was accepted by the six Northern Counties, who constituted a Parliament for Northern Ireland, the rest of Ireland refused to accept or act upon it. The Sinn Fein members of Parliament met in Dublin as *Dáil Eireann*, and declared an Irish Republic, formed a Government and took all possible steps to establish an independent administration. The country was at this time in a state of disorder, and some areas were placed under martial law. Large numbers of people were imprisoned or interned. In the summer of 1921 negotiations were initiated between the British Government and Mr De Valera with a view to arriving at an agreement, and arrangements made to hold a Conference in London in October. As a result of the Conference a treaty was framed and Articles of Agreement signed on December 6th, 1921, setting up an Irish Free State. A Provisional Government was formed, and in January 1922, the treaty having been ratified, took over control of Irish affairs.

A General Election was held on the 16th June 1922, a Draft Constitution in conformity with the treaty being published on the same day. A large majority of the members returned at the election were pro-treaty, but the meeting of the new Dáil was postponed owing to the state of the country. Religious and political animosity in the "six-county area" led to the shooting of numerous civilians, Catholic and Pro-testant, with raids along the border of this area. Over a wide area in Southern Ireland republican soldiers waged war against the forces of the Free State Govern-ment, and destroyed roads and bridges all over the country. Public and private buildings were destroyed —among them the splendid building of the "Four Courts" in Dublin with its priceless records. The regular army, however, drove the Republicans from the various towns and villages which had been held by them, and though, up to the latter part of August, guerilla warfare was carried on, normal conditions were being established over the greater part of the country.

EDUCATION

IRELAND has a system of education offering many points of interest, the result of a long series of attempts to bring educational policy and administration into harmony with the social and religious conditions of the country. Ireland at a very early period was renowned for her scholarship. For the three centuries after the coming of St Patrick it was a great centre of learning and civilisation, and deservedly acquired the title *Insula Sanctorum et Doctorum*. Its great schools of learning, which grew out of the monastic system, date from the middle of the fifth century. Early in the sixth century the celebrated School of Clonard in Meath was founded by St Finian, and afterwards followed those of Clonfert founded by St Brendan, Clonmacnois, Durrow, Kells, Bangor, and (about the year 636) the great School of Lismore on the Blackwater. These schools were frequented not only by the English nobility, but by scholars from the continent of Europe who flocked into Ireland to learn at the feet of those great masters whose fame had spread far and wide. But these schools were destroyed, and their books burnt during the Danish irruptions of the ninth century, their scholars seeking refuge in foreign countries.

The attempts made to anglicise Ireland and to implant English ideals, begun in the time of the Tudors, completed the work of destruction. First came the " grammar schools," then the beginnings of a " National " system of primary education about 1537, when parochial schools were established by the Irish Parliament. But the spirit pervading the attempt was alien. It succeeded in destroying the existing education but it did not succeed in its attempt to " reform " Ireland. Under Elizabeth, diocesan schools were established for the children of Protestants, while the schools established by the Irish Parliament were intended for the poorer Catholics. In 1608 " royal free schools " were established in the towns of Armagh, Cavan, Raphoe, Enniskillen, Dungannon, and Banagher, and some half a century later Erasmus Smith, an alderman of the City of London, gave lands for the purpose of establishing schools for the education of the poor children of Ireland. Grammar schools were founded at Galway, Drogheda, and Tipperary, and may be regarded as the equivalent of the primary schools of to-day. Increase in the rental of these lands enabled more schools to be established, and between 1808 and 1815 sixty-nine schools of this class opened under trust deeds, and between 1839 and 1843 the accumulation of a further surplus allowed of the establishment of fifty-two more. The schools were Protestant.

A further movement to establish Protestant schools was that of the " Incorporated Society for promoting

Kilkenny College

English Protestant Schools in Ireland " founded in 1733. It is clear that the aim of this and similar educational efforts of the period was to proselytise. This appears from the charter granted by George II to the Society. During the early part of the nineteenth century, associations were formed for the purpose of establishing schools and promoting education, but the aim involved proselytism. As Protestant schools, however, they have attained a high reputation.

In 1802 the " Order of Irish Christian Brothers " was founded in the city of Waterford by Edmond Rice. The members of the Order took vows of chastity, poverty, and obedience, and the object was the educattion of male children " according to the principles and teaching of the Catholic Church." They bound themselves to teach gratuitously. It has developed into a very important teaching organisation, not only in schools of a primary type, but also in the sphere of secondary education.

In 1807, and again in 1824, Commissions were appointed to inquire into Irish primary education. They both reported in terms favourable to undenominational teaching. These reports were in 1828 referred to a Select Committee of the House of Commons, which expressed the opinion that children of different denominations should be brought together for instruction in moral and literary knowledge, with facilities for separate instruction in religious knowledge where differences of creed made this necessary. Hence arose in 1831 a scheme for a National system of primary education in Ireland. The intention of the Government of the day was to bring about a mixture of denominations, but this was not realised.

The primary schools of Ireland are now controlled by a National Education Board consisting of twenty Commissioners, one of whom is the Resident Commissioner, who is generally responsible for the administration of the system. There are over 8000 schools with nearly 700,000 pupils, of whom about 75 per cent. are Roman Catholics. They are managed by different denominations, and afford combined literary and moral and separate religious instruction.

During the periods of " secular instruction " no emblems or symbols of a denominational nature may be exhibited in the schoolroom, but opportunities must be given to the pupils of all schools for receiving such religious instruction as their parents or guardians approve. In addition to the ordinary National schools there are some thirty " model schools " which are under the exclusive control of the Commissioners of National Education. The object of these schools was to afford models of what ordinary national schools should be, and they were provided with excellent buildings at the expense of the State. Six of the number are attended mainly by Roman Catholic pupils, the remaining twenty-four almost exclusively by Protestants. The aim was to provide education irrespective of religious denomination, and to educate candidates for the office of teacher. Speaking generally, the effort has failed, and most of the model schools are poorly attended in spite of their excellent equipment. Teachers are trained in training colleges, of which there are seven, one being managed directly by the Commissioners, five by Roman Catholic, and one by Protestant managers. There is a scheme for Evening Continuation Schools, but it has never been taken up widely.

In addition to the schools already mentioned, there are some five reformatory and sixty-six industrial schools. These are under the control of the Chief Secretary, and provide an excellent practical course of instruction.

Most of the secondary schools of Ireland—and there are over 300 of them—work in connection with the Intermediate Education Board— a body established by Act of Parliament in 1878. In that year, of every 100,000 Protestants in Ireland, 199 were receiving a secondary education, but of every 100,000 Catholics only two were being educated in the endowed secondary schools. The Intermediate Education Board was formed to promote intermediate secular education. A system of public examinations of pupils was established, on the results of which grants are made to the schools, and prizes and exhibitions granted to the pupils.

The Board now consists of twelve Commissioners

Clongowes Wood College

assisted by two paid Assistant-Commissioners. It is empowered to make rules which are subject to the approval of the Lord-Lieutenant. For many years the grants paid to schools under the rules were based solely upon the results of the examinations of their students, and there was no system of inspection. During the last few years, however, inspectors have been appointed, and important changes made in the rules.

The examinations of the Board are held at convenient centres in June, and exhibitions, medals, and prizes are awarded in the different grades as a result of the examinations.

Prior to the year 1900, there was no organisation for carrying out a comprehensive system of technical education in Ireland. There existed Science and Art classes conducted under the Science and Art Department of South Kensington, but there was nothing corresponding to the forward movement which had characterised the previous decade in England. Ireland's share of the local taxation duties paid to the local taxation account as a result of the passing of the Local Taxation (Customs and Excise) Act was not devoted to technical education as in England, but went to the support of elementary and secondary schools. It could hardly have been otherwise, for there was not in existence any local machinery capable of administering a system of technical education. County Councils were not established in Ireland before 1898. There was, however, a strong and enlightened spirit abroad, which led to the formation in 1895 of a Committee, formed during the parliamentary recess, and known as the Recess Committee, of leading Irishmen. The Report of this Committee, issued in the following year, led to legislation, and in 1899 there was placed on the Statute Book the Agriculture and Technical Instruction (Ireland) Act which established a new Department of State, and provided funds for agriculture and for technical education. It also

Technical School, Bolton St., Dublin

provided for the transfer to the new Department of a number of existing institutions already referred to. The new Department was endowed with wide powers, and very remarkable progress followed its establishment. The first Vice-President, Mr (now Sir) Horace Plunkett, and the Secretary, Mr. T. P. Gill, were respectively Chairman and Secretary of the Recess Committee. Associated with the Department are a Council of Agriculture, an Agricultural Board, and a

Board of Technical Instruction, the members of which are partly elected and partly nominated by the Department. The functions of the Boards are mainly advisory, but they control expenditure of the Department's endowment for technical instruction.

The first aim of the Department was to reform the teaching of Science in the secondary schools of Ireland.

School of Rural Domestic Economy, Westport

They issued a programme which was adopted by the Intermediate Education Board, and made full provision for the further training of secondary teachers. Almost every secondary school was provided with laboratories and suitable equipment for the teaching of Experimental Science. Summer courses for teachers were established in Dublin and at various provincial centres, and still form a strong feature of the Department's work. In connection with County and

Urban Councils, there were formed Committees of Agriculture and Technical Instruction. Schemes of technical education were framed and put into operation, and large numbers of students flocked into the schools and classes which were rapidly organised. Technical schools were built, while in the rural districts

A Butter-making class, Co. Wicklow

classes in manual work, domestic economy, and various forms of home industry were established under suitably trained itinerant teachers. On the agricultural side itinerant teachers were trained and appointed to work under local committees; these deal with various branches of agricultural work—poultry-rearing bee-keeping, fruit culture, butter-making, etc., while more recently winter agricultural classes have been organised. There are scholarship schemes which carry a boy from the elementary school to places of higher education, and a scheme of apprentice scholarships which provide a maintenance allowance throughout the whole period of apprenticeship, combined with attendance at a technical school. Another scheme provides, after two years' apprenticeship, a course of one year at specially

A School of Rural Domestic Economy,
Benada Abbey, Co. Sligo

organised higher courses of instruction arranged at a technical school. There are also a large number of scholarships for girls, securing for them a course of training in domestic economy, in one or other of the Residential Schools of Domestic Economy, working under the direction of the Department. The training of teachers of Science and Technology is carried out at the Royal College of Science, and teachers of

o

domestic economy are trained at the Irish Training School of Domestic Economy, St Kevin's Park, Kilmacud, a few miles from Dublin.

The Royal College of Science for Ireland is an institution for providing a higher training in applied science. It was established in 1867 on the recommendation of a Royal Commission. It is now housed

The Royal College of Science, Dublin

in a magnificent building in Upper Merrion Street, Dublin (opened by the King in 1911), and embraces three faculties, viz. Agriculture, Applied Chemistry, and Engineering. It has a large staff of professors and lecturers and awards a Diploma of Associateship.

The Albert Agricultural College at Glasnevin provides a training in agriculture for male students, while the Munster Institute at Cork is used for training female students in dairy work, poultry-rearing, etc.

The Department's work is also co-ordinated with that of the Congested Districts Board, and of the National Education Board, and includes courses of instruction for the further training of elementary school teachers in experimental science, drawing,

Albert Agricultural College, Glasnevin, Co. Dublin

school gardening, domestic economy, etc. Provision is also made in many technical schools for classes in domestic economy for pupils of National schools.

For over two centuries and a half Ireland had but one university—the University of Dublin. Now it has three. In 1591 Queen Elizabeth granted a charter incorporating Trinity College, Dublin. Although designated a college it was clearly intended to be a college of a university, though no other college has ever been created. Trinity College is for this reason frequently confused with the University of Dublin, of which it is the only college. The original charter conferred upon the Provost and Fellows the power to make statutes for the college, but in 1637 Charles I granted a new charter in which the Crown reserved the exclusive right of making statutes.

This splendid old university, which has given to the world such men as Hamilton, Burke, Goldsmith, Swift, and Berkeley has, from its foundation, been in the hands of Protestants, and though always attended by a certain number of Roman Catholics it failed to satisfy their demands. Prior to 1793 the college statutes required oaths such as Roman Catholics could not take, and up to 1873 the provostship, fellowships, and foundation scholarships could only be held by members of the Church of Ireland. Nevertheless, Trinity led the way in removing these disabilities, and more than half a century before the Test Act which admitted Nonconformists to membership of English Universities, the degrees of the University of Dublin were thrown open to the world. The government of the university is in the hands of the Provost and the seven Senior Fellows in conjunction with the Visitors. There is a Senate, and a Council consisting of the Provost and sixteen members of the Senate. There are twenty-four Junior Fellows. The faculties are in Arts, Medicine, Engineering, Law, and Divinity. Terms may be kept either by examination or by lectures. Except in the case of music, candidates for degrees in any subject must first graduate in Arts. The library of the university,

University College, Dublin

containing the Book of Kells and other treasures, is world-famed. It has also a University Press, Botanical Gardens, and an Astronomical Observatory at Dunsink. Women have been admitted to lectures, and examinations, and to degrees in Arts since 1904.

The scope of this volume does not permit of an account of the history of the controversy over the University question in Ireland, or of the changes which have from time to time taken place. The Queen's Colleges of Belfast, Cork, and Galway (an attempt to provide higher education of an undenominational character), and the Royal University (an examining body) are now things of the past, and ceased to exist as such when the Irish Universities Act of 1908 came into operation. This Act provided for the establishment of two universities, one in Dublin and the other in Belfast. A new college was to be founded in Dublin, while the Queen's Colleges of Cork and Galway were to be constituent colleges of the new National University. Handsome buildings for University College, Dublin, have recently been completed in Earlsfort Terrace. The New University though for a time handicapped (so far as Dublin was concerned) by want of adequate buildings, rapidly organised its forces, and students poured into its lecture rooms. Thus the " University question " which burned so long and so fiercely in Ireland has at long last ceased to exist.

In connection with education, reference must be made to the enlightened and far-reaching influence of the Royal Dublin Society, whose headquarters are in Leinster House. This Society had its origin in 1731, and had for its aims " improving Husbandry, Manufactures, and other useful Arts and Sciences." It soon became a medium for the administration of public funds for the encouragement of Science, Art, and Industry. It took steps which led to the establishment of the Royal Botanic Gardens at Glasnevin. The accumulation of books, models, and specimens marked the beginning of movements which resulted in the establishment of the Science and Art Museum and

National Library, Dublin

National Library. Statistical and industrial surveys of Ireland were initiated. The Irish Parliament entrusted the Society with the formation and management of drawing schools, and of a Museum of Natural History, and out of these efforts ultimately grew the Metropolitan School of Art (which now serves as a College of Art for the whole country), and the Royal College of Science for Ireland, to which reference has already been made. So far from having outgrown its usefulness the Society is still a vigorous influence, carrying out important educational, industrial, and agricultural work, to which reference will be made elsewhere, as also to the educational influence of the Royal Irish Academy and the Royal Hibernian Academy.

INDUSTRIES & MANUFACTURES

AGRICULTURE

IRELAND is, *par excellence*, an agricultural country. Its total area of 20,371,125 acres was in the year 1914 utilised as follows :

	Acres.
Barren mountain, turf-bog, marsh, town and building lands, roads, fences, water, etc.	2,814,480
Woods and plantations	296,800
Pasture, including grazed mountain . .	12,444,780
Corn crops	1,247,003
Green crops	1,015,406
Flax	49,253
Fruit	16,090
Hay	2,487,313

The outstanding feature of this table is the small proportion of land under cultivation, this being smaller than the average for the United Kingdom, and considerably smaller than the proportion in any country in Europe with the exception only of Norway and Sweden. The area of land under cultivation has for over half a century steadily diminished, and this shrinkage is not peculiar to Ireland alone of the countries of the

United Kingdom, but it is nowhere so marked as in Ireland. The area under cultivation has continuously decreased while the grass lands have correspondingly grown. An examination of agricultural statistics for past years shows a general and rapid decrease in cereal and green crops. Thus in 1851 the area under corn

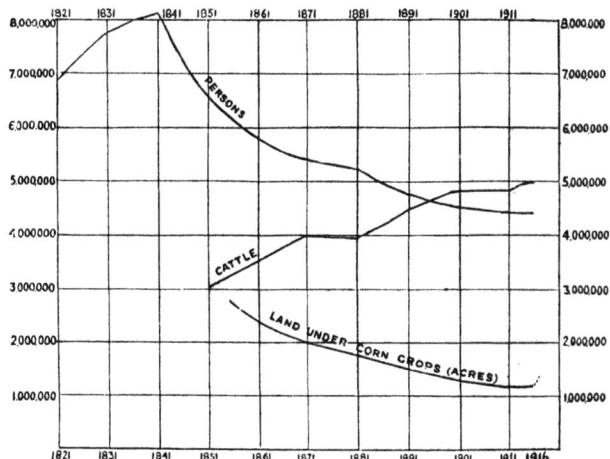

Relation of Population to Cattle and Corn

crops was 3,099,401 acres ; this had decreased to 1,247,003 acres in 1914. With the urgent demand for home-produced food supplies during the war, and the measures adopted by the Department of Agriculture and Technical Instruction to encourage and enforce cultivation a great increase of tillage took place. The maximum was reached in 1918 when there were 5,709,912 acres under the plough, of which 1,932,793 acres were under corn crops. Green crops and flax occupied

1,513,142 acres in 1851 decreased to 1,068,786 acres in 1913 but rose to 1,288,199 acres in 1918. In the same period (from 1851 to 1913) the area under hay had increased from 1,246,408 to 2,481,822 acres since which it has not greatly changed. It is, however, interesting to observe that the *rate* of decrease in the area under corn had rapidly diminished prior to the war. Between 1851 and 1913 the decrease was 59.2 per cent.

Raising and Packing Potatoes, Clonakilty

while the decrease between 1904 and 1913 was only 1.2 per cent. The most noteworthy decrease among the cereals is in wheat which decreased from 504,248 acres in 1851 to 34,004 acres in 1913. This decline was most marked in Leinster and Munster. The acreage of potatoes also heavily declined since 1861. In that year there were 1,133,504 acres under potatoes but this decreased to about one half by 1913; the acreage rose to 709,263 in 1917. Flax also is a crop of which the acreage has declined. In 1851 there were 140,536 acres under flax—in 1913 there were only 59,305 acres almost wholly in Ulster. Owing however to the cutting off of foreign supplies of flax during the war, and the huge demand for aeroplane linen a great impetus was given to the cultivation of flax, and in 1918 the area under flax rose to 143,355 acres. It was reduced to 95,610 acres in 1919, but rose to 127,198 acres in 1920. Experiments on the growing and curing of tobacco have been made during the last few years, and have been attended with a certain measure of success.

Fruit is a crop of increasing importance owing to the improved organisation for its better cultivation and marketing. In 1913 there were 15,734 acres of fruit, of which over half was in Ulster. It rose to nearly 20,000 in 1919. The Department of Agriculture and Technical Instruction have done much in recent years to improve the quality of the fruit grown as well as to secure better grading and marketing.

It will cause no surprise to find that with the striking decrease in tillage the population of Ireland has continuously and steadily declined. In England such a change in the usage of the soil has involved migration from countryside to town—in Ireland it has involved emigration, principally to the United States of America.

If we turn our attention to live stock we observe a marked contrast. With a decline in population there has been a continuous increase in the number of cattle, accompanied by a marked improvement in their quality. The number of cattle increased from nearly three millions in 1851 to close upon five millions in 1913. There has been a large increase in sheep and horses. There were in 1854 over one and a half millions of milch cows in Ireland, and slightly over one million six hundred thousand in 1913; but the proportion of milch cows to the total number of cattle has steadily decreased. There is an enormous increase in poultry.

Large numbers of horses, cattle, sheep, and pigs are exported from Ireland every year. No fewer than

An Irish Hunter

21,481 horses, 768,491 cattle, 586,968 sheep, and 65,854 pigs were exported to Great Britain and the Isle of Man in 1921.

In the butter industry, and the poultry and bee-keeping industries enormous improvements have taken place during the last decade. The Department have, through their various schemes, encouraged all forms of agriculture, and the industries just quoted yielded an immediate return.

A question of primary importance is the distribution of land, and the size of the holdings. There were in 1917 as many as 572,574 holdings. Nearly half of these were of an area not exceeding 15 acres and only 1967 exceeded 500 acres. An outstanding feature of recent

The Munster Institute, Cork

years has been the increase in the number of holdings between 15 and 100 acres.

Increasing attention is paid to the question of afforestation. Of the total area of Ireland about 1.4 per cent. is under woods. The woods in England are 5.2 per cent., in Scotland 4.5 per cent., and in Wales 3.9 per cent. of the total areas.

Agricultural education has steadily developed, and in addition to the agricultural schools situated in various parts of the country, the Department carry out a scheme

Clonakilty Agricultural Station

Agricultural Station, Ballyhaise, Co. Cavan

of winter agricultural classes. The training of dairy-maids and instructresses in dairy work, poultry rearing, etc., is carried on at the Munster Institute, Cork, and other training centres. The interests of farmers have been fostered by an important organisation — the Irish Agricultural Organisation Society —

Killeshandra Co-operative Society, Co. Cavan

which seeks to secure among other objects co-operative action among farmers. The shows held under the auspices of the Royal Dublin Society have proved a powerful stimulus to the horse and cattle-breeding industries.

The conditions which followed the outbreak of war brought out in a striking manner the importance of Ireland as a food-producing country. Before the war agriculture had responded to the efforts made by the Department through education and in many other ways to improve the practice of farming. Both the quantity and the quality of its output of food supplies had been enormously improved before the outbreak of war, and by 1913 its supply of food and drink stuffs imported

Roscommon Hogget Rams

into and retained for consumption in Great Britain had reached a point where it was only exceeded by that of one other country in the world—the United States of America. In the year referred to the value was for Ireland thirty-six millions, and for the United States thirty-nine millions. Ireland is, in an increasing degree, an essential base, not only for the British food supply but also for British agriculture, whose meat-raising and dairying depend greatly on Ireland's breeding and production. Although having only 10 per cent. of the population, Ireland produces 40 per cent. of the cattle and 30 per cent. of the pigs of the United Kingdom. She consumes only one-fourth of her own cattle—the rest are for Great Britain. Of the beef-cattle, two out of every five killed in Great Britain were bred in Ireland.

During the war the difficulty of ocean transport rendered the maintenance of food supply a most difficult problem, and a Defence of the Realm Regulation made it obligatory on any occupier holding more than 10 acres of arable land to cultivate at least 10 per cent. of the arable area of his holding in addition to the amount under cultivation in 1916. The response of farmers was spontaneous, and the exercise of the compulsory powers almost unnecessary. Within the space of three months a total new area of 637,000 acres was brought under the plough and put under food crops. With the conclusion of the Armistice, and the resumption of the normal food supply much of this cultivated area is going back into pasture.

FISHERIES

The sea fisheries of Ireland have for centuries been a source of livelihood to the coast dwellers, and to the people of Western Europe generally. The Scandinavians who, for centuries before the Anglo-Norman invasion, occupied the coast towns of Ireland profited by the fish which crowded its waters, and in the fifteenth and sixteenth centuries Spaniards fished off the west coast. Philip II paid £1000 into the Irish Treasury for permission to fish on the Irish coast, and in the reign of

P

Charles I the Dutch were granted a licence to use
the Irish Fisheries on payment of £30,000. In the
seventeenth century the French were the principal
fishers. Schemes to suppress foreign fishing, and to
encourage it as a native industry were launched from
time to time.

In the latter half of the eighteenth and the early part
of the nineteenth century the activity in the fisheries
was promoted by means of bounties, but this artificial
inflation ceased with the withdrawal of the bounties in
1829. The rapid increase in the population of Ireland
which reached a maximum about the middle of last
century, led to the vigorous working of the Irish fisheries
by the native population. Cod, ling, hake, and herrings
were caught in abundance and cured to meet the
local demand. The tide of prosperity commenced to
ebb after the great famine in 1846, after which the
population fell from eight to less than six millions
during the decade. When this phase had passed a
new set of conditions appears—the introduction of
steam-power was revolutionising society. The ac-
celerated means of transit greatly quickened the demand
for fresh fish, and hundreds of boats flocked to Kinsale,
Baltimore, Berehaven, and Valencia, to the mackerel
fishery. This development was greatly facilitated by
loans issued by the Inspectors of Fisheries—including
one made by the Baroness Burdett-Coutts—to enable
the fishermen to get modern boats. These loans were
well repaid. In 1899 the office of Inspectors of Fisheries
was incorporated with the new Department of Agriculture and Technical Instruction, and this Department
became the central authority for the Irish fisheries.
A great change took place in the nineties in the intro-

duction of steam as a motive power for trawlers, liners, and drifters. This application of steam has been of restricted value to Irish fisheries, as the extensive trawling grounds lying to the south and the south-west of Ireland, where hake, ling, megrim, haddock, and bream form the bulk of the catch, are exploited almost exclusively by English-owned steam trawlers, which land their fish in English ports. More recently the use of paraffin motor engines has been adopted, and steps taken by the Technical Branch of the Department to train the men in the use of such engines.

Concurrently with these developments has been the improvement of harbour accommodation rendered necessary by the advent of the steam drifter and big motor craft. Among the other duties of the Fisheries Branch of the Department is the protection of the fisheries and the enforcement of the bye-laws. This is assisted by their fishery cruiser, the *Helga*, which has not only repressed illegal trawling but is of use in connection with the scientific investigations in regard to fisheries.

On the rocky western coast of Ireland, exposed to the full fury of the Atlantic, fishing is often impossible for long periods. The east coast, however, offers shelter and fishing ground of moderate depths, and hence we find from Belfast to Kinsale fishing communities who make sea-fishing their life-work. On the west coast, except in some favoured localities, fishing is carried on by " crofter " fishermen rather than by concentrated fishing communities. These men have holdings of land, and their interests are divided between the land and the sea. Their equipment is simple and takes the form of row-boats or canvas canoes, good enough when the fish come close in as they always do in certain seasons. One advantage at all events of these canvas boats on this storm-beaten shore is that they can be lifted by their crews well out of reach of

Fishing Coracles on the Boyne, Drogheda

the heavy seas—seas that have been known to smash lighthouse walls 200 ft. above sea-level.

The fishing grounds around Ireland yield sole, turbot, cod, haddock (which disappeared from Irish inshore waters for some twenty years, returning again in large quantities) herring, mackerel, plaice, and

other varieties in smaller quantity.   Hake which used
to provide a valuable fishing on the south coast have
now almost ceased to visit the inshore waters.   Plaice
fishing in Ireland, in contrast to the conditions found
in the North Sea, and, to a less extent on the west coast
of England, is confined to the shallow bays.   The deep

"Black Hookers"

trough and muddy bottom of the Irish Sea forms a
barrier to the seaward extension of the fishery, though
several fish marked in Irish bays have crossed to the
English and Welsh coast, and the reverse journey has
occasionally been made by fish with English labels.
The fish are very unequally distributed both in space
and time.   The various classes of fish mentioned have
their favourite haunts, but they are inconstant, for

what reasons is not known. Shoals of mackerel come with fair regularity twice a year and give rise to the spring and autumn mackerel fisheries, the spring fishing being mainly a large boat fishery, while the autumn is mainly a row-boat and canoe fishery. Some of this fish finds its way fresh to the English markets, but the bulk of the trade is with America, the curing being carried on at a number of centres. The total value of the Irish mackerel fishery was in 1913, £52,735. (In 1912 it was £77,859.) The vessels use drift-nets, but the best quality of pickled mackerel sold in the United States is derived from fish caught on hand lines in the North Sea and cured on board the fishing-boats. It may be noted that the Irish mackerel fishery for 1918 was the best for many years past, the autumn yield was higher than for twenty years. The total yield of the spring and autumn fisheries was 493,000 cwts. of the value of £520,000.

The herring fisheries show very great fluctuations, and the cause of this is not fully understood. It is a universal phenomenon, however, and is generally supposed to be due to the occurrence of exceptionally good spawning seasons at irregular intervals. These increase the stock of fish, and thus start a profitable fishery which lasts until that particular stock is exhausted. While in 1908 the total quantity of herrings landed during the winter fishery was under 160,000 cwts., in 1910 it amounted to nearly half a million cwts. The total quantity of herrings landed during the summer herring fishery of 1920 amounted to 184,000 cwts. as compared with 155,000 cwts. landed in the corresponding season of 1919. Notwithstanding this decline in the total weight, the value of the catch was estimated at about £93,000 which shows an increase of nearly £13,700, as compared with 1912. The more important collecting stations are Howth and Ardglass, the latter place having attained some importance as a curing port. Herrings are kippered at Howth and Dunmore East.

Lobsters are found in large numbers wherever the coast is rocky, and there are good oyster beds, which the Department have sought to improve by restocking.

There were 4319 vessels with crews numbering 15,677 persons engaged in fishing in the year 1920. The use of motor fishing vessels is extending. There were thirty-six such vessels in use in 1910, and the number had increased to 539 in 1920.

A comparatively recent development is the establishment of two Whaling stations in Mayo—at Inishkea and Blacksod. Over a hundred whales were landed in 1913.

Irish inland fisheries are of considerable importance. The inland salmon fishery is of great value. Some 12,000 professional fishermen are engaged in it, and it is carried on largely at or near the mouths of rivers ; drift-nets and draft-nets or " seines " are used. The Danish seine or " ring net " as it is now called in Ireland, is an efficient implement in shallow water, and was first made known to Irish fishermen through the agency of the Department. Its use is rapidly extending on the east coast. Sea trout, or white trout, as they are called in Ireland, are of great value on the west coast, while brown trout are in almost every lake and stream, so that Ireland offers unusual facilities for anglers. Great attention is paid by the Department to the preservation and improvement of the inland fisheries, and they make grants for this purpose to the various Boards of Conservators.

MANUFACTURES

Though Ireland's staple industry is agriculture, it has developed other important and prosperous industries in the face of great difficulties. The value of these are best estimated from a consideration of the value of our import and export trade. The records of the trade in manufactured goods are compiled on a voluntary basis, and cannot be regarded as satisfactory, but the figures as far as can be ascertained are suitable for comparison, and are as follows : Ireland's export of manufactured goods in the year 1904 amounted to the value of $15\frac{1}{2}$ million pounds—her import of such goods in the same year was 25 million pounds. In the year 1914 the values (estimated at 1904 prices) were : Exports, 24 millions ; Imports, nearly 29 millions. The figures for the war period show a reduction, and they may be passed over as abnormal. The vitally important fact is that in the decade referred to, the value of the manufactured exports have increased by some $8\frac{1}{2}$ million pounds, while the *excess* of imports over exports has decreased from $9\frac{1}{2}$ million pounds to less than 5 million pounds. This indicates most encouraging industrial progress.

In spite of her slender resources of coal and iron, Ireland has built up one of the largest shipbuilding industries in the world, and a huge and flourishing linen industry. It will be observed that these great industries are largely concentrated in the " north-east corner," which is wealthy and prosperous. Coal is imported from Scotland for the northern counties, and from Lancashire for the central and southern counties. There are a few coal mines working on the coalfields, which yield principally an anthracitic coal. Those of the Leinster coalfield yield anthracite alone, while the northern coalfields of Lough Allen (Arigna) and Eastern Tyrone produce a bituminous coal. Serious efforts were made during the war to develop the Irish coalfields. A railway has been constructed to connect the Queen's County Collieries with the Great Southern and Western main line at Athy, and another to connect the Castle-comer Collieries to the Waterford Branch at Dunmore,

White Star Liner *Olympic*

near Kilkenny. As for iron, it may be said that the iron-ore associated with the Coal Measures of North Kerry and Clare was smelted in the seventeenth century. In 1672 about a thousand tons of iron was made in Ireland. In Antrim iron-ores are found associated with the basaltic rocks. Something like 41,000 tons were produced in 1914.

The shipbuilding industry of Belfast is a triumph of business organisation and mechanical skill. The coal and iron required must be imported, yet the industry has until recently flourished greatly. It had its beginning in the days of wooden ships — as far back as 1636—and the firm of Harland & Wolff are now at the head of the world's shipbuilding industry. This firm turn out the huge and stately liners of the White Star Company, and have supplied machinery for some of the largest vessels of the British Navy. The gross tonnage of the vessels they build annually approaches the huge total of 100,000. Indeed, in 1919, the gross tonnage launched by this firm amounted to 110,190, though this fell to 82,110 in 1920, the falling off being partly due to the fact that many thousands of men were released from ship construction to recondition the liners released by the Admiralty after war service. There are other factors which militated against rapid construction. They employ a large number of men, at times as many as 16,000, but at present the industry is suffering from a world-wide depression in shipbuilding.

The firm of Messrs Workman & Clark come next, being one of the largest shipbuilding firms in the world. They have built steamers for the Cunard Company, the Allan Line, the Norddeutscher Lloyd, the Hamburg-American, and other lines. This firm launched six steamers with a gross tonnage of 34,433 in 1920 as compared with thirteen with a gross tonnage of 87,636 in the previous year. In recent years successful efforts have been made to develop the shipbuilding industry in Londonderry and Dublin, and vessels of moderate size have been launched from these yards. Larne also has a small shipbuilding industry. The estimated total value of steam vessels exported from Ireland in 1904 was £1,500,000 ; in 1913 it was £3,148,000 ; and in 1920 it was £12,720,000.

The linen industry of the north is no less remarkable.

It was carried on as far back as the thirteenth century. In 1739 the export of linen from Ireland amounted in value to over £600,000 and, though it was seriously threatened at the end of the eighteenth century by the cotton industry, which attained considerable success, its prosperity was renewed when the spinning of flax

A Flax Scutching Machine

by machinery was introduced—the cotton industry declined in a corresponding manner. The industry was for a time encouraged by bounties. Notwithstanding many vicissitudes and fluctuations it attained a highly flourishing state, though it has necessarily suffered most severely from the industrial depression and social up-heaval which followed the war and still persists. It has a large market in the United States, in spite of the very

heavy tariff on linen goods. Little flax was grown in
Ireland prior to the war, that used coming mainly from
Belgium. A great impetus was given to the cultivation of
flax during the war owing to great demand for aeroplane
linen, and to the cutting off of foreign supplies. The
effort continued, and over 127,000 acres were under
flax in 1920, but fell to about 40,000 in 1921. The export
of linen goods in 1913 was valued at over £14,000,000,
and this rose to £40,500,000 in 1920. The shirt-making
industry, of which Londonderry is the centre, is of great
importance, and affords employment to a large number
of women and girls in the surrounding districts.

The woollen industry is more generally distributed
over the country. Irish homespuns have for long
enjoyed a well-deserved reputation, but the growth
of power-driven factories is gradually making inroads
on the hand-loom industry which is, however, still an
important industry in Donegal and other western
counties. Since the war, efforts have been made to
resuscitate home-spinning, with some success. The
export of woollen goods showed a marked increase
in the years previous to the outbreak of war. The
Irish woollen mills are generally small, and have not
the advantages which attach to a large organisation.
The industry is, however, indigenous, and flourished
greatly in the past until repressive legislation checked
its development. It is now progressing, and with improved design and some combination between producers
now happily secured, there is every reason to antici-
pate that it will again become a great industry. Owing
to wool scarcity during the war manufacturers were
driven to use Irish wool where previously they had
used imported yarn. It was found suitable where it

had been thought to be unsuitable, and more home-grown wool will, it is hoped, be used by Irish manu-facturers. The manufacture of carpets has shown a marked increase, and the decade preceding the war saw increased activity in many branches of industry.

Ireland has for long been famed for her home in-dustries, particularly those of an artistic character, and

Ballydougan Machine Embroidery School,
Gilford, Co. Down

strenuous efforts have been made to conserve and further develop these. The lace and crochet industries are widely distributed, and in many districts have been an important supplementary source of income to poor families. The making of crochet, and the various descriptions of lace properly so-called, such as Carrick-macross, Limerick, Needlepoint, etc. has been encouraged and improved through the efforts of the Congested Districts Board and the Department. Teachers have been trained, and classes formed and maintained in many parts of the country. The School of Art in Cork has for long played an important part in this work of training, and lace design is now taught in all the schools of

Machine Embroidery School, Maghera,
Co. Londonderry

art so that the design of lace and crochet has much improved. Hand embroidery is also a noteworthy industry. In the counties of Down, Londonderry, Donegal, and Fermanagh, among others, it is extensively carried on. The more simple kind of embroidery is known as " sprigging," and employs a large but diminishing number of home workers. One reason for the decline has been the growth of the machine embroidery industry in Switzerland and Germany.   Much Irish linen has in the past been sent to Switzerland to be embroidered on machines, with a consequent loss of employment to hand-workers in Ireland.   The Department, however, established two schools of machine embroidery, one at Ballydougan in Co. Down, the other in Maghera in Co. Londonderry.   These have proved very successful, and a large number of machines are now in use in the north of Ireland.   The machines are operated by hand, and the work is carried on under pleasant and healthy conditions.   The schools were managed by linen firms, and their absorption into the industry provided for.   It seems more than probable that the vast bulk of the work previously done by hand will come to be done on machines of this type though high-class distinctive work will still employ the skilful and experienced hand-worker.

INDUSTRIAL RESOURCES

Minerals.—Mineral mining is carried on in various parts of the country, but not on an extensive scale, and its mineral resources have never been properly developed. Ireland possesses many valuable marbles and building stones.   Its beautiful green Connemara marbles are well known, and the black limestone marble of Kilkenny has been quarried for many years.   The granites of the Wicklow hills are quarried in various places for building and ornamental purposes, and also for paving setts.   Barytes is worked in Co. Cork at the Duneen Bog Mines, Clonakilty, and at the Dunmanus Bay Barytes mines near Ballydehob.   Ochre is worked in the Vale of Ovoca (Co. Wicklow).

Near Toome and Portglenone in Co. Antrim a

material called Diatomite or Kieselguhr has for some years been won. It occurs at the surface as a stratum of white soft silicious material. It is made up of the silicious " tests " of countless millions of microscopic organisms known as diatoms. Kieselguhr has been largely used as an absorbent in the manufacture of explosives, but is also used for heat-insulating purposes. Carbide of calcium (made from lime and anthracite or coke) is manufactured at Collooney in Co. Sligo, and Askeaton in Co. Limerick. Bauxite has been mined in Antrim. At Larne a factory was established by the British Aluminium Company for the separation of the alumina from bauxite, the alumina being then sent to the Fall of Foyers in Scotland for the extraction of aluminium. The French bauxite was, however, found more suitable, though bauxite is still largely exported to England for use in the chemical industries there.

Many minerals remain to be profitably developed in the future. Excellent glass sands are, for example, to be found in large deposits on Muckish Mountain, Co. Donegal. Materials suitable for the manufacture of Portland cement exist in several localities, and there has already been established a factory at Magheramorne, near Larne (Co. Antrim), with a capacity of from forty to fifty thousand tons per annum. The cement is made from chalk quarried in the neighbourhood and clay dredged from the adjacent lough. Cement is also manufactured on a smaller scale near Drinagh in Co. Wexford.

But when the fullest account has been taken of the existing industries, and of the progress which has already been made, it is quite clear that Ireland is backward industrially. It is only necessary to compare its in-

A Biscuit Manufactory

dustrial output with that of Scotland to realise at once
the backwardness and the opportunity which co-exist.
This is not the place to enter into an analysis of the
causes of this industrial backwardness, but one cause
falls within the scope of this sketch of Ireland's industrial position. The replacement of manual labour
by mechanical power in manufacturing processes has
led to the steady progressive decline of hand and home
industries, and industries have tended to concentrate
in areas where fuel for power purposes could be obtained
cheaply. Ireland imports nearly all the coal she consumes. Her imports of coal amount to over $4\frac{1}{2}$ million
tons per annum, but the output of her mines, which
amounted to about 149,000 tons in 1854, has declined,
and the average output for the ten years 1909–1918
amounted only to some 88,000 tons. The actual output
in 1918 was 92,001 tons (the annual output in Great
Britain is about 250 million tons). When to the cost
of imported coal is added that of inland transport,
the cost of steam power became a serious handicap to
its use. It is true that Ireland has enormous deposits
of another fuel, less valuable than coal but, from its
wide distribution, and because of the comparative ease
with which it can be won, is of the greatest actual and
potential value to the country. Ireland's peat deposits,
at present used almost entirely as a domestic fuel over
the greater part of the country, seem destined to serve
a wider purpose. There is also to be considered the
water power which may be derived from her rivers
and loughs. The failure to use these great natural
sources of energy for industrial purposes is to be attributed largely to the fact that they are situated in places
remote from populous and industrial centres, and it

does not, except in exceptional circumstances, pay to take an industry to a power site, especially when that is in a sparsely populated district. But a new factor has been introduced into the problem. This factor is the ease with which mechanical energy can be converted into electrical energy and this, after transmission at high pressure, with slight loss, to considerable distances, reconverted into mechanical energy. This fact, which is of the utmost significance in relation to Ireland's industrial development, justifies a short account of the three great natural resources referred to.

Coal.—The proved Irish coalfields occupy an area of somewhat more than 110 square miles, and the thickness of the seams is not considerable. The actual reserves of coal are estimated at over 180 millions of tons.[1] Of this over 8 million tons are in the Lough Allen (Arigna and Slieve-an-Ierin) area, about 157 million tons are in the Leinster field, and about 15 million tons in the Tipperary (Slieveardagh) field. The coal in the southern area is anthracite, that in the northern area is semi-bituminous in character.

There are certain other coalfields small in extent at Ballycastle (Antrim), and in Co. Tyrone (Coalisland, Dungannon, and Annaghone). The amount of coal in these fields remains to be proved. At Ballycastle there is probably some 14 million tons, and the Lower Coal in Tyrone probably contains 31 million tons. The extent of the Middle Coal is unknown. It will be seen that our coal reserves are not considerable, but it is remarkable that the output is so meagre. This may be attributed in part to the absence of transport facilities, and in part to the cost of winning. The seams

[1] Irish Coal Industry Committee (1919).

are so thin that, in order to win a ton of coal, much rock must be removed. This accounts to a large extent for the circumstance that the annual output per underground worker in Ireland is only 149 tons, while in Great Britain it is 294 tons.[1] A consequence is that wages tend to become low, that a shortage of labour results, or, if they are increased, the owners would find themselves unable to compete with output from mines in Great Britain. The higher wages in Great Britain, increased cost of sea transport, and improved railway facilities to Irish mines are favourable to increased output in Ireland. It has been seen that the great bulk of Irish coal—that of the Leinster coalfield, is anthracite. This is a hard, bright, clean coal containing nearly 94 per cent. of carbon. It has little ash or volatiles, and has a high calorific value. It has been used very largely for domestic heating in the districts surrounding the mines, but it possesses certain defects. It is hard to light, and is almost flameless. It remains burning for a long time, and may be used in anthracite stoves with great economy and satisfaction. It is also satisfactory for use in gas producer plant.

Peat.—The domestic fuel, *par excellence*, over the greater part of Ireland is peat, and this, happily, is widely distributed over its surface, of which it occupies over three million acres. As the total area of Ireland is over twenty million acres, it will be seen that the peat bogs occupy one-seventh of the surface. They vary in size from the vast Bog of Allen to small detached mountain bogs, on which the peasantry have " turbary rights," and which have served as their sole source of fuel for centuries. In many places, indeed, the small

[1] Irish Coal Industry Committee, 1919 (Cmd. 650)

bogs have been entirely cut away, and the consequent dearth of fuel offers a serious problem in such districts. But while the larger bogs have been cut along their margins, their outlines have been little changed during the course of a century, as may be seen by an examination of the maps in the monumental Report of the Bogs Commissioners appointed in 1809 " to enquire into the nature and extent of the several bogs in Ireland, and the possibilities of draining and cultivating them."

The greater portion of the surface under turf bogs occurs in a wide belt crossing the middle of Ireland from east to west, commonly overlying the low-lying limestone strata of this region. They are the result of certain topographical and meteorological conditions, the chief of which appear to be stagnant water and a humid climate. In these conditions, reeds, cotton grasses, heather, and sphagnum mosses grow rapidly. The accumulation and decomposition of this leads to the formation of peat, the growth above and decomposition below going on concurrently. The dead vegetable matter loses its more volatile constituents which are given off, the " marsh gas " sometimes becoming ignited, and producing those wandering lights or *ignes-fatui*, popularly known as *Will-o'-the-wisp* or *Jack-o'-the-lantern*. With the loss of these constituents the mass turns to a brown and ultimately to a black colour, and in time deposits accumulate to a depth of 40 ft. or more. The average depth of the flat bogs of the central belt is estimated at 18.66 ft.

Perhaps the most consistent and baffling quality of the peat bogs is their amazing and ineradicable wetness. In an undrained bog the peat contains from 90 to 95 per cent. of water, and efficient drainage does

not reduce this below 88 per cent. The peasantry
of Ireland cut this wet mass into sods or turves by
means of spades of special shape, called "slanes."
These sods are spread over the surface of the uncut bog to
be dried by the air and sun during the summer months,
and are then carted to the homestead or farm and
stacked. It is estimated that each family using turf
as fuel uses on the average as much as 25 tons in the
year. In a good season it may be dried to 25 per cent.
moisture-content, when it is collected and stacked for
winter use. Fortunes have been spent in attempts to
dry peat artificially, but so far without economic success.
The moisture cannot be removed by pressure, for it is
held in a gelatinous or colloidal state which defies
pressure, and, though there are methods of breaking up
the fibre and expelling the water, it is not yet clear
that the process is profitable from an economic standpoint. As a fuel, peat may be said to have a calorific
value varying from one-half to two-thirds that of coal.
A fair sample of peat of 25 per cent. moisture yields
7,370 British thermal units. The corresponding value
of a sample of Wigan coal was 13,300 units, and of
Castlecomer anthracite, 14,931.

It is estimated that the peat bogs of Ireland contain
no less than 3700 million tons of *dry* or *anhydrous*
peat. It also appears from careful estimates that the
consumption of peat for domestic purposes in Ireland
amounts to as much as 7,000,000 tons per annum,
which may be considered equivalent to 3,500,000 tons
of coal. It seems, therefore, that the peat resources
of Ireland could not only supply this need, but replace
the imported coal for a period of two hundred years!
But peat is a bulky, friable fuel, difficult to transport,

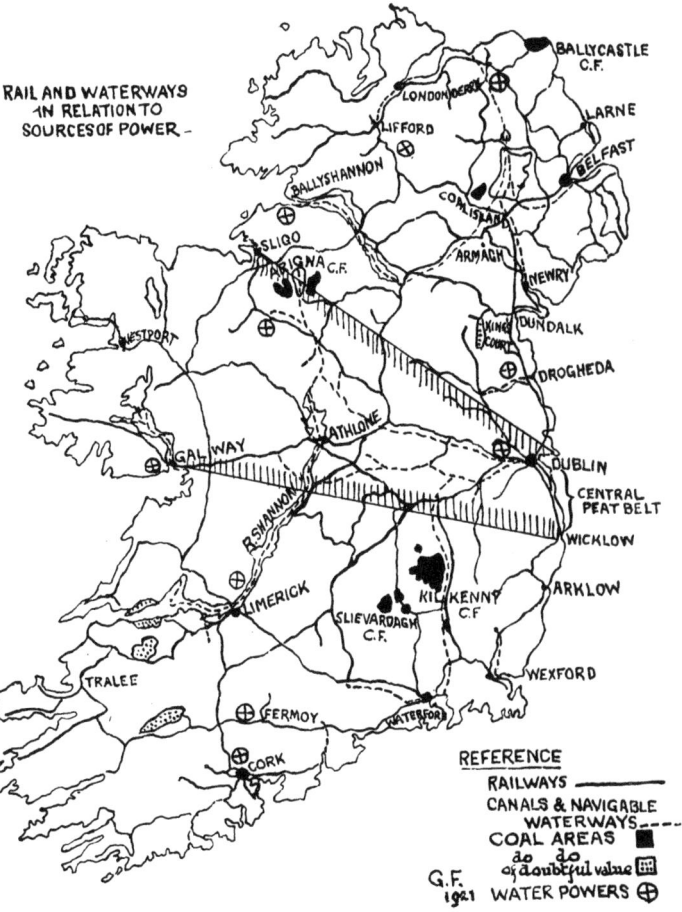

RAIL AND WATERWAYS
IN RELATION TO
SOURCES OF POWER -

BALLYCASTLE
C.F.

LONDONDERRY
LARNE
LIFFORD
BELFAST
BALLYSHANNON
COALISLAND
SLIGO
ARMAGH
ARIGNA C.F.
NEWRY
WESTPORT
KINGS
COURT
DUNDALK
DROGHEDA
ATHLONE
GALWAY
DUBLIN
CENTRAL
PEAT BELT
R. SHANNON
WICKLOW
LIMERICK
KILKENNY
C.F.
ARKLOW
SLIEVARDAGH
C.F.
TRALEE
WEXFORD
FERMOY
WATERFORD
CORK

G.F.
1921

REFERENCE
RAILWAYS
CANALS & NAVIGABLE
WATERWAYS
COAL AREAS
do   do
of doubtful value
WATER POWERS

and not well-suited to industrial uses. It has, however, been used successfully in gas-producer plant, and it seems not improbable that it will be found feasible to use it in such plant in the neighbourhood of the bog, and employ the gas for gas-engines, which will in turn drive dynamos. The electric current may then be used for industrial purposes, *e.g.* electro-chemical industries in the neighbourhood, or transmitted at high pressure to industrial centres. It must be noted that the ammoniacal by-products of the peat are of considerable value as a source of nitrogenous manures. The nitrogen-content of Irish bogs averages about 1.8 per cent. This compares favourably with that of other countries.

Water Power.—As in the case of peat, the achievements of the electrical transmission of power have given a new significance to the problem of utilising the power at present running waste in our rivers. It has been assumed by the great majority of people that the absence of large waterfalls, such as characterise Switzerland and Norway, indicates a paucity of water power in Ireland, the surface contour of which appears at first sight unfavourable. The general contour is that of a shallow bowl or plate—a large central plain of slight elevation with short seaward slopes. In point of fact these conditions are by no means unfavourable. The great natural loughs afford storage so that by the construction of suitable barrages the water engineer can store the water in the wet season, and use it in the dry season, and so secure not only a more uniform distribution of power throughout the year, but also an improvement in drainage conditions, inasmuch as the tendency to flooding is enormously reduced by he regulation of outflow.

It is also a useful fact that the " fall " is generally confined to a limited section of a river. Thus, while above Killaloe there is a fall of only 55 ft. in 125 miles of the Shannon, there is a fall of over 90 ft. between that point and Limerick.

It is scarcely possible to estimate with any degree of accuracy the total amount of water power which

The Rapids, Leixlip, Co. Dublin

might be obtained from Irish rivers. Such an estimate might be arrived at either from daily measurements of the flow of its rivers spread over a sufficiently long period, or calculated from the rainfall in each catchment area, with corrections for evaporation, losses, etc. With the exception of several of the large rivers which have been systematically " gauged," such measurements of flow are not available, while the rainfall records are very imperfect. Attempts have from time to time been made by Sir Robert Kane and others to estimate the power which might be obtained from Irish rivers, and it seems clear that over 500,000 horse power could be developed *continuously*. The question

Sluices near Carrick-on-Shannon, Lough Allen

of the development of these resources has been investigated quite recently by the Irish Water Power Resources Sub-Committee, which was appointed in November 1918, by the Board of Trade, and reported in 1921.

There are scattered over the country a number of small water-power installations, as at Sligo, Newry,

Lucan, Galway, and on many of the northern streams
and rivers, but the total power so developed is but a
small fraction of that which could be obtained by the
application of comprehensive schemes directed to the
development of each river basin as a whole. It is, of
course, a fact that there are other interests which must
be conserved, such as fisheries, navigation, drainage,
and potable supplies, but quite consistently with the
conservation of these interests it is abundantly clear
that a huge power could be developed and made available for industrial purposes, that industry could be
supplied with cheap power and Ireland's import of coal
enormously reduced. Not only could the larger rivers,
such as the Shannon, Erne, Lower Bann, and Liffey be
" harnessed," but a large number of the smaller rivers
also. It is possible too that tidal power may be used,
as at Strangford Lough, though the problems involved
in its utilisation are more difficult than in the case of
the rivers. It is certain that water power, combined
with electrical transmission, will play a very important
part in Ireland's industrial future.

DISTINGUISHED IRISHMEN

Within the limited space available, it has only been
possible to notice a few representative names in
various departments of human activity, preference
being given to those whose work it is believed has
helped to mould and influence the thought and actions
of their countrymen. With the exception of St Patrick,
only Irishmen have been included. Dignitaries and

office holders, as such, have had to be excluded, also many great names belonging to the princely families of the different provinces : O'Neills, Maguires, O'Conors, O'Briens, O'Sullivans, FitzGeralds of Kildare and of Desmond, Butlers of Ormond, etc., which play so conspicuous a part in the history of Ireland. The great heroes of antiquity whose exploits have been handed down in the national epics : Conchobar, Cúchulinn, Fergus, Cúrói, Ailill, Medb, etc., have had to be passed over. Of the numerous saints, poets, and scholars of ancient Ireland only a few could be mentioned. Actors, painters, and engravers, who perhaps have less influence upon a community than poets and men of action, are given but sparingly. On the other hand it has been thought that those who devoted their lives to the study of the history, topography, and antiquities of Ireland, should in a work of this nature receive more than a passing mention.

BALFE, Michael William (1808-70), operatic composer, born in Dublin, commenced the study of music when five years old. Left to his own resources at sixteen, he went to London and played as a violinist in the band at Drury Lane Theatre. Subsequently he went to Italy, and studied singing and counterpoint at Rome and Milan. Visiting Paris in 1828, he met Rossini, who gave him an engagement as baritone singer in the Italian Opera there. Returning to Italy he produced his first opera at Palermo (1829), and others in quick succession at Pavia and Milan, while continuing to sing on the Italian stage until 1835. Back in London, he began his brilliant career as a writer of English operas with *The Siege of Rochelle*, produced at Drury Lane, 1835. His fame was now securely established, and he continued to delight the public by new and attractive works. His *Maid of Artois* (1836) contained one of the most popular of English songs, " The Light of other Days." From 1840–5 he was in Paris, where he brought out fresh works at the Opéra Comique. The most famous of all his operas, *The Bohemian Girl*, was produced when on a visit to London in 1843. From 1845–52 he was conductor at Her Majesty's Theatre, in succession to Costa. Afterwards he visited Berlin, Petrograd, Trieste, and Paris, where he was received with enthusiasm and loaded with honours. In 1864 he retired to a property in Hertfordshire. He was a prolific and spontaneous composer, possessing a rare gift of melody.

BERKELEY, George, Bishop of Cloyne (1685–1753), the philosopher, was born near Thomastown, Co. Kilkenny, and educated at Trinity College, where he became a Fellow in 1707, and held several lectureships. In 1713 he went to London, and became intimate with Swift, Addison, Steele, and Pope, contributing to *The Guardian*. Afterwards he spent several years abroad. In 1724 he was appointed to the rich Deanery of Derry, but almost immediately returned to London with a project for establishing a college in the Bermudas for the civilisation of America. Having procured a charter and a vote of £20,000 from parliament, he sailed with his young wife and several friends in 1728. He landed at Newport, Rhode Island, where he built a house, and there spent three. years awaiting the promised support, which not being forthcoming, he returned to London, having sunk his private fortune in the enterprise. In 1734 he was consecrated Bishop of Cloyne ; he refused the Primacy in 1745. Towards the end, failing health led

him to retire to Oxford, where he died six months later.
He is buried there, in Christ Church Cathedral.   One of
the most acute intellects of the age, Pope attributed to
him " every virtue under heaven."   His chief works,

George Berkeley, Bishop of Cloyne

distinguished for their literary style no less than their
profound thought, are : *Principles of Human Knowledge*
(1710) in which he postulated that matter had no existence apart from the conceiving mind ; *Three Dialogues
between Hylas and Philonous* (1713) ; *Alciphron* (1732) ;
Theory of Vision (1733), and *The Querist* (1735–7), in

which he anticipated the political economy of Hume, Adam Smith, and Ruskin.

BOYLE, Hon. Robert (1627–91), natural philosopher and chemist, was born at Lismore Castle, the fourteenth child of the "great" Earl of Cork. He was educated at Eton under Sir Henry Wotton, and abroad, at Geneva, Florence, and Paris, from 1638–44. On his father's death (1644) he inherited the manor of Stalbridge, Dorset, which he made his home, and also estates in Ireland. He devoted himself to science, and was one of the originators of the Royal Society. On returning from a visit to Ireland in 1654 he settled at Oxford, where he erected a laboratory, and carried out extensive experiments on air and respiration, by means of his improved air pump, known as "machina Boyleana." These he described in his first work, *New Experiments Physico-Mechanical* (1660); in the second edition (1662) he announced his discovery that the volume of a gas varies inversely as the pressure, known as "Boyle's Law." His *Sceptical Chymist* (1661) gave the death blow to alchemy, and laid the foundations of modern chemistry, giving the true definition of a chemical "element." He left Oxford for London in 1668, where he took an active part in the meetings of the Royal Society, of which he declined the presidentship (1680), and also repeated offers of a peerage. A devout Christian, he was able to read the Bible in Hebrew, Greek, and Chaldee, and he spent large sums in the diffusion of the Scriptures; among other versions, he bore the expense of Bedell's Irish translation. By his will he founded the "Boyle Lectures" to demonstrate the truth of Christianity. His *Works* were collected by Birch, in five folio volumes, in 1744.

BRIAN of Bórumha (941–1014), High-king of Ireland, was son of Cennetigh, chief of the Dál Cais. In 964, when Mathgamhain, Brian's elder brother, succeeded to the throne of Cashel, the Danes held all the chief fortresses of Munster. Brian urged his brother to rise against them, and collecting their forces they overthrew the Danes at Sulcoit in Tipperary (968), and regained possession of Limerick. In 976 Mathgamhain was assassinated at the instance of Maelmhuaidh, king of Desmond, and was succeeded by Brian, who two years later defeated Maelmhuaidh at the Battle of *Bealach Leachta*, and thus became king of all Munster. Having formed an alliance with Maelseachlainn, king of Meath, and High-king of Ireland, he inflicted a crushing defeat on the Danes of Leinster at *Glenmama* in Wicklow (999), and seized their stronghold, Dublin. He then made an alliance with Sitric, their king, and assuming the high-kingship (1003) gradually extended his rule over the other provinces, but confirmed Armagh in its ecclesiastical supremacy (1005). His reign was marked by great prosperity. He restored the ruined monasteries, built bridges and forts, and revived the arts. At length the Danes rose against him, summoning to their aid forces from Scandinavia and the Isles. Brian defeated them with great slaughter at *Clontarf* on Good Friday, 1014, and by this decisive battle broke the power of the Danes in Ireland. He himself was slain at the end of the day by a fugitive Dane, and was buried at Armagh.

BURKE, Edmund (1729–97), the great statesman and political philosopher, was born in Dublin, and educated at Ballitore School and Trinity College. In 1750 he went to London and entered the Middle Temple, but was never called. His *Vindication of Natural Society*, a satirical imitation of Bolingbroke, and his essay on *The Sublime and Beautiful* (1756) introduced him to the literary celebrities of the day, Dr Johnson, in particular,

Edmund Burke

whose intimate friend he became.   In 1759 he projected *The Annual Register*, which he edited for some years. For a time (1761–4) he acted as secretary to "Single-speech" Hamilton, Chief Secretary for Ireland.   In

R

1765 he was for a brief period private secretary to Lord Rockingham, first lord of the Treasury, and entered parliament for Wendover. He subsequently sat for Bristol (1774–80), and Malton (1780–94). The corruption and abuses of the North administration inspired some of Burke's noblest utterances : his speeches on "American Taxation" (1774), "Conciliation with America" (1775), and his famous *Letter to the Sheriffs of Bristol* (1778). He was for a short time paymaster-general in two administrations in 1782–3. The remainder of his political life was devoted to the affairs of India. His impeachment of Warren Hastings in 1788 ranks as one of the greatest orations of all time. The most widely known and influential of his writings is *Reflections on the French Revolution* (1790), to the principles of which he was violently opposed. On the death of his only son Richard, he retired from political life, an annual pension of £3700 being settled upon him. He died at Beaconsfield, and is there buried.

COLUMBA, Saint (521–97), better known by his Irish name Columcille, "Dove of the church," the greatest of Irish saints, was born at Garton in Donegal, of royal descent, his father, Feidlimid, being a great-grandson of Niall of the Nine Hostages, and his mother, Eithne, eleventh in descent from Cathair Mór, King of Leinster. He studied at the celebrated monastic schools of Finnian of Moville [*q.v. Ulster* volume], and Finnian of Clonard [*q.v. Leinster* volume]. Columba founded many churches and monasteries in Ireland, of which the most important were Derry (546), Durrow in Kings Co. (553), the head of the Columban institutions, and Kells in Co. Meath. In 563 he left Ireland, an exile, according to tradition, on account of his share in the battle of

Culdreimhne (561), and sailed to the island of Hy (Iona), off the coast of Argyllshire. There he built a monastery, and in 565 set out on his successful mission to the northern Picts under King Brude, who were still pagans, and the inhabitants of the western isles. Iona gradually became a great centre of missionary activity. From it Aidan (d. 651), who has been called the real apostle to the English, rather than Augustine, went forth in 634 to found the church of Northumbria. Columba re-visited Ireland on several occasions, notably in 575, when he attended the great Convention of Drumceat. He died at Iona. Three Latin hymns are attributed to him, and a number of beautiful Irish poems, which are however linguistically later. He was a consummate scribe. A sixth-century copy of the Psalms traditionally ascribed to him, and known as the *Cathach*, is still preserved. The chief authority for his life is Adamnan [*q.v. Ulster* volume].

COLUMBANUS, Saint (543–615), the great missionary to the Franks and Lombards, was born in Leinster. After spending many years in the monastic school of St Comgall at Bangor [*q.v. Ulster* volume], he set out about the year 585 on his mission to Gaul. He settled down in Burgundy, where he founded monasteries at Anegray, Luxeuil, and Fontaines. Here by his pious zeal and austere practices he attracted great numbers of converts. His *Rule*, which was of the strictest nature, became an object of veneration, and was observed conjointly with that of Benedict in many Gaulish monasteries to the middle of the seventh century. Having by his uncompromising moral attitude incurred the displeasure of Brunhild, he was forced to leave Burgundy in 610. Making his way up the Rhine,

he passed through Switzerland, where his companion,
Gallus, founded the monastery of St Gall, and came into
Lombardy. Here in 613 he founded the monastery,
afterwards so celebrated, of Bobbio, where he died
shortly afterwards. Columbanus adhered to the Celtic
usages in the celebration of Easter, the tonsure, etc.,
and defended his views in correspondence with Popes
Gregory the Great and Boniface IV. Besides his
Epistles, he wrote a *Penitential*, a *Commentary on the
Psalms*, and several poems. His works were collected
by Patrick Fleming (1599–1631), a native of Louth,
whose *Collectanea* is now of extreme rarity. His life
was written by Jonas, who entered Bobbio a few years
after the saint's death.

FOLEY, John Henry (1818–74), the sculptor, was born
in Dublin, and studied in the schools of the Royal Dublin
Society and the Royal Academy, London. In 1839 he
exhibited his first work, *The Death of Abel*, and in the
following year his classical group *Ino and Bacchus*,
which made his name widely known. His *Youth at the
Stream* (1844) led to a commission for the statues of
Hampden and *Selden* in Westminster Hall. He was
elected an A.R.A. in 1849, and an R.A. in 1858. His
three equestrian statues in bronze of *Lord Hardinge*,
Lord Canning, and *Sir James Outram*, in India, are said
to be his finest works, and the best equestrian statues
of the day. He was chosen by Queen Victoria to do
the group *Asia* and five of the emblematic figures for
the *Albert Memorial* in Hyde Park, also the figure of
the Prince Consort. Among other famous portrait
statues by him are *Lord Clyde*, in Glasgow ; *Stonewall
Jackson*, in the United States ; *Lord Herbert*, in Pall
Mall ; *John Stuart Mill*, on the Embankment ; *Sir*

Charles Barry, in Westminster Hall ; the beautiful bronze statues of *Goldsmith* and *Burke* in front of Trinity College, Dublin ; *Lord Gough*, in Phœnix Park ; and the *Father Mathew* monument at Cork. Famous groups are *Caractacus*, and *Egeria* in the London Mansion House, *The Mother*, and the *Death of Lear*. One of the greatest of modern sculptors, he is buried in St Paul's Cathedral.

GOLDSMITH, Oliver (1728–74), poet, essayist, and dramatist, was born at Elphin, Co. Roscommon, the son of a poor clergyman, who moved to Lissoy shortly after his birth. He graduated at Trinity College, and in 1752 entered the University of Edinburgh as a medical student, completing his studies at Leyden in 1754. For two years he wandered on foot through Holland, France, Germany, Switzerland, and Italy as a strolling musician. Settling in London in 1756, he passed eight years in great poverty, in turn physician, apothecary's assistant, usher, and bookseller's hack, until he attracted the notice of Dr Johnson by his *Chinese Letters* (1760), afterwards republished as *The Citizen of the World*. He then became a member of the celebrated Literary Club, in which Johnson, Burke, Reynolds, and Boswell were the leading spirits. His beautiful poem, *The Traveller* (1765), and his delightful tale, *The Vicar of Wakefield* (1766), placed him in the front rank of men of letters. In 1768 his comedy, *The Good Natur'd Man*, was produced at Covent Garden, and in 1773, *She Stoops to Conquer*, the gayest and most delightful of English comedies, only rivalled by Sheridan's *School for Scandal*, produced four years later. His second great poem, *The Deserted Village*, the companion to *The Traveller*, appeared in 1770. Reckless and improvident, Goldsmith was forced to squander his exquisite talent in compila-

tions for which he lacked the requisite knowledge—
*The Roman History, An History of the Earth and Animated
Nature*, etc., which however lacked none of his accustomed
charm and grace of style. " Let not his frailties be remembered," said Dr Johnson, " he was a very great man."

GRATTAN, Henry (1746–1820), one of the greatest of
Irish statesmen and orators, was born in Dublin, his
father being Recorder and member for the city. On
leaving Trinity College, he entered the Middle Temple,
London, and in 1772 was called to the Irish Bar. In
1775 he entered the Irish parliament as member for
Charlemont, and joined the opposition. Largely owing
to his efforts the restriction acts which were in force
since the reign of William III. were repealed. In 1780
he began his great struggle for the legislative independence of Ireland, by a memorable speech in which he
maintained " that the king, with the lords and commons
of Ireland, were alone competent to enact laws to bind
Ireland, and that Great Britain and Ireland are in-
separably united under one sovereign." The Act of
Repeal, passed two years later, gave Ireland the independent parliament sought for. For his signal
services in obtaining this great concession, parliament
voted Grattan £50,000. He subsequently lost popularity
for a time by his opposition to Flood's demand for a
special Act of Renunciation, which was actually passed
by the English parliament in 1783. All his efforts were
henceforth directed to parliamentary reform and Catholic
emancipation. Disappointed by the opposition he
encountered, and broken in health, he retired from
parliament in 1797. After the Rebellion he returned as
member for Wicklow, and employed all his eloquence in
opposing the Union. In the Imperial parliament he

devoted his remaining energies to Catholic emancipation. Crossing over from Ireland in an exhausted condition with a petition to parliament in its favour, he
succumbed in London, and was buried in Westminster
Abbey.

HAMILTON, Sir William Rowan (1805-65), mathematician, was born in Dublin. At an early age he gave
proof of his extraordinary talents, having acquired
when still a boy a knowledge of thirteen languages,
including several oriental. As a mathematician he was
almost entirely self-taught. When nineteen he read a
paper before the Royal Irish Academy on *Caustic Curves*,
which he recast and published three years later as
Theory of Systems of Rays (1827). In a third supple-
ment (1833) he predicted, on theoretical grounds, the
law of " conical refraction," afterwards verified experi-
mentally at his request by Humphrey Lloyd, thus
establishing the undulating theory of light. While still
an undergraduate he was appointed to the Chair of
Astronomy in Trinity College, and he shortly afterwards
became Astronomer Royal. The publication of his
next great work *General Methods in Dynamics* (1834),
setting forth the principle of " varying action," caused a
sensation in the mathematical world, and won him
European fame. His *Algebra considered as the Science
of pure Time* (1835) led to his greatest achievement, the
invention of quaternions, described in 1843 in a paper
Researches respecting Quaternions (1847), a new method
of dealing mathematically with the science of space,
and more fully in *Lectures on Quaternions* (1853). He
was President of the Royal Irish Academy (1837–46),
and an honorary member of several European Academies,
including that of St Petrograd. His literary attain-

ments were also of a high order ; he was the friend and correspondent of Wordsworth, Southey, and Coleridge. He was knighted in 1835.

JOHANNES SCOTUS (c. 817–877), the philosopher, sometimes called *Erigena*, was a native of Ireland. About the year 845 he migrated to France. Charles the Bald appointed him professor in the school of the palace at Laon, where there was a colony of Irish scholars. In 851 at the instance of Hincmar, Archbishop of Rheims and Pardulus, Bishop of Laon, he wrote his *De Præ-destinatione* in reply to Gottschalk. His bold and rationalistic views were however condemned by the synods of Valence (855) and Langres (859). One of the few competent Greek scholars in the West, he was commanded by Charles to translate the works of the pseudo-Dionysius the Areopagite. His translation is still extant, also several commentaries on his author. His great work *De Divisione Naturæ*, written in the form of a dialogue about 867, revealed him as one of the subtlest and most original thinkers of the age. In this memorable work of neo-Platonic speculation he sought to reconcile the truths of Christianity with human reason, the supremacy of which he always maintained. It was condemned by Honorius III. for its pantheistic tendency. His teaching had a powerful influence on mediæval thought down to the time of Anselm. Other writings of his still extant are *Commentaries on Martianus Capella*, and *Boëthius*, and a translation of the *Greek Ambigua of St Maximus*, also poems in Latin and Greek, several in praise of his patron Charles, with whom he lived on terms of familiarity. He died probably in France, though a later tradition has connected him with Malmesbury.

LECKY, William Edward Hartpole (1838–1903), the most distinguished of Irish historians, was born at Newtown Park, near Dublin, and educated at Trinity

W. E. H. Lecky

College. His literary beginnings, which were anonymous, excited no interest, and brought him disappointment, particularly his *Leaders of Public Opinion in Ireland* (1861), remarkable essays on Swift, Flood, Grattan, and

O'Connell. This work he considerably recast, and re-
issued in 1871 and 1903. Fame was, however, not long
delayed. It came on the publication of his *History of
Rationalism* (1865), a work of immense learning, which
at once introduced him to the highest literary circles in
London. His *History of European Morals from Augustus
to Charlemagne* (1869) added to his reputation. He
then married and settled in London, devoting all his
energies to the *History of England in the Eighteenth
Century* (1878–90), his greatest work. The soundness of
judgment displayed in these volumes, no less than the
wide learning and scrupulous impartiality, made a
profound impression, especially in the portion relating
to Ireland, re-issued separately as *History of Ireland in
the Eighteenth Century* (5 vols.). His other works
include *Democracy and Liberty* (1896) and the *Map of
Life* (1899). A liberal in politics he supported the dis-
establishment of the Irish Church, but was opposed to
Home Rule. From 1895–1902 he represented Trinity
College in parliament. He received the Order of Merit
in 1902.

MACLISE, Daniel (1806–70), historical and *genre*
painter, was born at Cork, the son of a Scotch father and
an Irish mother. He studied at the Cork Academy,
and opening a studio, maintained himself by drawing
portraits in pencil. With his savings he went to London,
and scored a success by a lithograph of Charles Kean as
"Norval." In 1828 he entered the schools of the Royal
Academy, and soon carried off the principal prizes. In
1829 he exhibited his first picture at the Academy,
Malvolio and the Countess. In the following year he
began his celebrated series of portraits of literary
celebrities in *Fraser's Magazine*, over the signature

" Alfred Croquis." His success was rapid. By his splendid banquet scene, *The Chivalric Vow of the Ladies and the Peacock*, he secured his election as A.R.A. (1836), becoming a full member four years later. On the death of Sir Charles Eastlake in 1866, he was offered, but declined, the Presidentship. Among his more celebrated pictures are *Christmas in the Baron's Hall* (1838), *Play Scene in Hamlet* (1840), *Marriage of Eva and Strongbow* (1854). His fame, however, rests on his frescoes in the Houses of Parliament, *The Meeting of Wellington and Blucher* (1861) and the *Death of Nelson* (1864), which cost him seven years of arduous labour and many disappointments. These splendid works, in which his defects as a colourist are not so apparent, entitle him to rank as the greatest historical painter of the British school.

MANGAN, James Clarence (1803–49), poet and essayist, was born in Dublin. His father being unsuccessful in business, he was removed from school at fifteen, and apprenticed to a scrivener, serving years of depressing drudgery. About 1838 he received employment in the Ordnance Survey Department under Petrie [*q.v. Leinster* volume], and on its breaking up was given temporary employment in the Library of Trinity College by Dr Todd. His last years were passed in misery and ill-health, brought on largely by his intemperate habits. He died in the Meath Hospital of cholera, it is said, and was buried in Glasnevin Cemetery. A drawing of him on his death-bed was made by Sir Frederick Burton. Mangan's work was contributed to Dublin newspapers and periodicals, the bulk of it, no less than 500 poems and numerous prose essays, appearing in the *Dublin University Magazine*, for which he began to write in

1834.   His finest work is that inspired by Gaelic originals, such as *Dark Rosaleen*, the poem on which his fame chiefly rests ; *O'Hussey's Ode to Maguire ; Ward's Lament for the Princes of Tirconnell ; Patrick Sarsfield*, etc.   Here he is the most truly national of Irish poets, and the precursor of the Celtic revival.   Only one collection of his poems appeared in his lifetime—*Anthologia Germanica* (1845).   A few months after his death O'Daly published his *Poets and Poetry of Munster*.   The first edition of his poems was edited with a fine appreciation by John Mitchel [*q.v. Ulster* volume] in 1859.

MOORE, Thomas (1779–1852), the most famous of Irish poets, was born in Dublin.   He was one of the first Catholic students to enter Trinity College, where his intimate friend was Robert Emmet (1778–1803).   In 1799 he went to London, and there his musical gifts soon made him a society favourite.   His *Odes of Anacreon* (1800), dedicated to the Prince of Wales, established his reputation as a poet.   In 1803 he went out to Bermuda as Admiralty registrar, but left for the United States the following year, appointing a deputy in his place. On his return to London he published *Epistles and Odes* (1806), and the year after began to issue his *Irish Melodies*, with airs arranged by Stevenson, the work which has brought him world fame.   They continued to appear until 1834, bringing him in over £12,000. *Lalla Rookh* (1817), an oriental poem, for which he received the unprecedented payment of £3000, was hardly less successful.   In 1818 Moore's deputy having absconded with £6500, he went abroad with Lord John Russell in order to avoid arrest, and spent the next few years in France and Italy, visiting Byron at Venice, who gave him the MS. of his *Memoirs*, which Moore subsequently destroyed.   His *Letters and Journals of Lord Byron* (1830) is his finest prose work.   A *History of Ireland* (1835–46) for which he too late discovered his unfitness, undermined his health and spirit.   He died at Bromham, near Devizes, which he had made his home since 1817, and is there buried.   His *Memoirs, Journals, and Correspondence*, were edited by his friend Lord John, afterwards Earl Russell (1853–56).

O'CONNELL, Daniel (1775–1847), the " Liberator," born near Cahirciveen, Co. Kerry, was educated at a Catholic school near Queenstown, and at St Omer and Douai.   He was called to the Bar in 1798, and rapidly acquired an extensive practice, his fees amounting some years to as much as £9000.   Throwing himself into the movement for Catholic emancipation, he successfully opposed (1814) the proposed Government veto in the appointment of Catholic bishops.   On the death of Grattan he was recognised as the leader of the Catholic party ; he founded the Irish Catholic Association in 1823.   His powerful efforts, and his election to parliament for Co. Clare in 1828, led to the passing of the Emancipation Act in the following year.   He took a leading part in the great political measures of the next ten years, and then entered upon his great struggle for the Repeal of the Union.   In 1840 he founded the Loyal National Repeal Association, and three years later organised monster meetings throughout the country, the most famous at Tara, where he addressed upwards of 250,000 people.   The meetings were suddenly proclaimed by the Government, and O'Connell, tried for seditious conspiracy, was heavily fined and imprisoned. The judgment was reversed by the House of Lords, and O'Connell was released ; but he never recovered his old spirit : the Famine and the New Ireland movement, which favoured revolutionary methods, broke him down. Ordered abroad by his physician, he died at Genoa, on

Daniel O'Connell

his way to Rome.   His remains were brought home and interred at Glasnevin Cemetery, Dublin.

O'DONOVAN, John (1806–61), Irish scholar, was born at Atateemore, Co. Kilkenny.   He began the study of

Irish when about nine years of age. In 1830 he entered the Historical section of the Ordnance Survey, super-intended by George Petrie, [*q.v. Leinster* volume], where he was employed in collecting material from ancient Irish MSS. in the Dublin libraries for the surveys of the various counties, and in determining the correct nomenclature for the maps, visiting the different localities for this purpose. This national work was stopped by the Government (1843) when only one volume, *London-derry*, had been published. The results of O'Donovan's labours are preserved in his invaluable *Ordnance Survey Letters*, now deposited in the Royal Irish Academy. In 1849 he was appointed professor of Celtic at Queen's College, Belfast, continuing to reside in Dublin. From 1852 he was engaged with O'Curry, at the Government expense, in preparing for publication the *Ancient Laws of Ireland*, a vast undertaking which neither lived to see published, their work being edited by others. The most eminent of Irish scholars, and the greatest of topographers, O'Donovan lives by his monumental edition of the *Annals of the Kingdom of Ireland, by the Four Masters* (1848–51) [*q.v.* O'Clery, *Ulster* volume], his *Irish Grammar* (1845), and the numerous editions of Irish texts contributed by him to the Irish Archæo-logical and Celtic Societies, covering almost every field of ancient Irish literature. In 1848 he received the Cunningham Gold Medal from the Royal Irish Academy, and was made a corresponding member of the Prussian Academy (1856). His death, after a few days' illness, was felt to be a national calamity.

O'NEILL, Hugh, second Earl of Tyrone (*c.* 1540–1616), one of the greatest of Irish statesmen and soldiers, was a grandson of Conn O'Neill (d. 1559) and nephew of the famous Shane O'Neill (*c.* 1500–67). He was brought up by Sidney at the court of Queen Elizabeth, and was for a time in her service, being present at the Smerwick Massacre in 1580, and aiding Essex in his Ulster wars.

Hugh O'Neill, Earl of Tyrone

Various reasons eventually led him to renounce his allegiance—the kidnapping and imprisonment for three years in Dublin Castle of his brother-in-law Hugh Roe O'Donnell, the oppression of the Catholics, and the growing encroachment of the English settlers upon the hereditary domains of the Irish chieftains. Upon

O'Donnell's escape he took up arms against the Queen, overthrowing her forces in several battles, his defeat of Bagenal (1598) at the *Yellow Ford*, near Armagh, being the greatest reverse the English had ever sustained in Ireland. Hugh Roe, then Earl of Tirconell, commanded the cavalry on this occasion. Having failed in 1602, owing to treachery, to raise the siege of Kinsale, and having submitted to Mountjoy, O'Neill made peace with the Queen. James I confirmed him in his title and possessions. On learning however that a false charge of conspiracy had been made against him and Rury, Earl of Tirconell, and being unwilling to share the fate of Shane O'Neill and Hugh Roe O'Donnell (d. 1602), the two Earls resolved on flight, and in 1607, set sail secretly from Lough Swilly with their families, one hundred persons on board. Passing through France and also Flanders, where they were hospitably entertained, they made their way to Rome, and were welcomed by Pope Paul V. There in the following year O'Donnell died, and O'Neill in 1616, blind and broken by misfortune.

PARNELL, Charles Stewart (1846–91), Irish political leader, was born at Avondale, Co. Wicklow, and educated at Magdalene College, Cambridge, which he left without taking a degree. In 1875 he entered parliament for Meath, as a follower of Isaac Butt (1813–79), leader of the Home Rule party, whom he succeeded in 1880. In his maiden speech he maintained that " in the neglect of the principles of self-government lay the root of all Irish trouble " ; and to attain this end all his efforts as president of the Land League, National League, and leader of the Irish party were henceforth directed. Though the Home Rule Bill introduced by Gladstone

S

in 1885, with his support, was not carried, Parnell, by his powerful "opposition" and brilliant leadership succeeded in effecting great reforms for Ireland. The

Charles Stewart Parnell

publication in *The Times* newspaper (1887) of facsimile letters purporting to be written by Parnell, and implicating him in certain political crimes, was denounced by him in the House, and led to the appointment of

the " Parnell Commission " (1888–89) to investigate
the charges. The letters were proved to be forgeries,
and Parnell was completely vindicated. He subsequently recovered £5000 damages from *The Times*. In
this historic trial Parnell was defended by his brilliant
countryman, Sir Charles Russell (1832–1900), afterwards
Lord Russell of Killowen, Lord Chief Justice of England.
Edinburgh conferred the freedom of the city upon him
in 1889. In 1890 he lost his influence greatly, owing to
certain divorce proceedings in which he figured, and
died shortly afterwards at Brighton.

PATRICK, Saint (*c.* 389–461), apostle to the Irish, was
a native of Bannaventa, a village by the sea, variously
held to be Dumbarton on the Clyde, and a village in
Glamorganshire. He was originally called Succat, his
father Calpurnius, a Briton, being decurion of the place,
and a Christian deacon. In his seventeenth year,
Patrick was captured by Irish freebooters and carried
into captivity in Ireland, where he served as a herd near
the forest of Fochlad, in the north-west of Connaught,
near Crochan Aigli. Another tradition places the scene
of his captivity in Antrim. After six years he escaped,
and embarking on a trading vessel reached Gaul. He
spent some years in the monastery of Lérins, and thence
passed to Auxerre, where he was ordained, and remained
many years. From here (432) he set out on his mission
to Ireland, consecrated by Germanus, in succession to
Palladius. Landing at Strangford Lough, he founded
his first church at Saul, near Downpatrick. He next
established communities in Meath, and thence pro-
ceeded to the conversion of Connaught. About 441–3
he is said to have visited Rome, shortly after his return
founding the church of Armagh, the primatial see (444).

He died and was buried at Saul.   His authentic writings
are his *Confession*, written in old age, and his *Letter
against Coroticus*, the ruler of Strathclyde.   The earliest
accounts of Patrick are the memoir of Tírechán, about
664–70, and the *Life* by Muirchu, son of Cogitosus,
about 699.   These and other interesting documents
relating to the saint are preserved in the early ninth-
century Book of Armagh.

ROBERTS, Sir Frederick Sleigh (1832–1914), Earl
Roberts of Kandahar, Pretoria, and Waterford was
born at Cawnpore in India, where his father General
Sir Abraham Roberts, a native of Waterford, held a
command.   He was educated at Eton.   He served
through the India Mutiny, winning the Victoria Cross
at Khudaganj.   In the Afghan War (1878–80), he
commanded the Kuram field force, and won fame by
his celebrated march to the relief of Kandahar (1880).
For this memorable achievement he was made a baronet
and given the chief command in Madras.   In 1885 he
was appointed Commander-in-Chief in India.   In 1892
he was raised to the peerage, and three years later
promoted Field-Marshal.   He was commander of the
forces in Ireland from 1895–99.   After a series of
British reverses in South Africa, culminating in the
disaster at Colenso (Dec. 1899), where his only son fell,
Roberts was sent out as Commander-in-Chief, with Lord
Kitchener as his chief of staff.   Immediately after his
arrival, the whole course of the war changed, and Roberts
having entered Bloemfontein and Pretoria, and annexed
the two South African Republics, returned home within
twelve months.   For his brilliant services he was
created an earl, voted £100,000 by parliament, and
made Commander-in-Chief of the British Army, in

succession to Lord Wolseley [*q.v. Leinster* volume].
When the European War broke out he emerged from
his retirement and gave his services, dying in France
when on a visit of inspection to the Indian troops
at the front.   He was the author of several works,
the best known being *Forty - one Years in India*
(1897).

SHERIDAN, Richard Brinsley (1751–1816), dramatist
and politician, was born in Dublin, his father Thomas
Sheridan being the well-known actor and author, while
his mother was .an accomplished writer, whose *Sidney
Biddulph* was described by Fox as " the best novel of
our age."   The family having removed to England in
1758, he was educated at Harrow.   He married Miss
Linley the singer in 1772.   Three years later he produced
his first great comedy *The Rivals* at Covent Garden,
also *The Duenna*, with music by his father-in-law.   In
1776 he became part-proprietor and manager of Drury
Lane Theatre, and in the following year produced *The
School for Scandal*, the wittiest and most brilliant comedy
in the English language.   Two years later he brought
out his last play, *The Critic*.   His intimacy with Fox,
Burke, and other public men led him into politics, and
in 1780 he entered parliament for Stafford   He was an
under-secretary of State in 1782, and Secretary to the
Treasury in 1783.   His greatest political achievement
was his speech on the Begum of Oude (1787), during the
impeachment of Warren Hastings, described by Burke
as " the most astonishing effort of eloquence, argument,
and wit united, of which there was any record or tradition " ; and Fox and Pitt were no less enthusiastic in
their praise.   In 1799 he became a privy councillor and
Treasurer to the Navy.   The burning of Drury Lane

Theatre (1809), which he had acquired and rebuilt, involved him in financial ruin. Disaster now overtook him ; he lost his seat in parliament (1812), and died not long afterwards in extreme poverty. He was given a public funeral in Westminster Abbey.

SWIFT, Jonathan (1667–1745), satirist and divine, was born in Dublin, of English parentage, and educated at Kilkenny School and Trinity College. In 1689 he became private secretary to Sir William Temple, at Moor Park, Surrey, with whom he remained until his death in 1699, save for an interval of eighteen months (1694–5) spent at Kilroot, near Carrickfergus, a living to which he had been presented. In 1700 he was appointed Vicar of Laracor, near Trim, but resided mostly in London. Here he soon acquired a great reputation by his brilliant satires *The Tale of a Tub* and *The Battle of the Books*, published anonymously, like almost all his works, in 1704. In 1713 he received the Deanery of St Patrick's as a reward for his great services to the Tory party. Henceforth his life was passed in Dublin. In 1724 he achieved a great popularity in Ireland by his *Drapier's Letters*, protesting against the patent granted to Wood, an Englishman, for the coinage in Ireland of £108,000 in halfpence, which he maintained would bring ruin upon the country. In his fourth letter he asserted the independence of Ireland, and that " government without the consent of the governed is the very definition of slavery." As a result the monopoly was universally condemned and had to be withdrawn. His most widely known work is *Gulliver's Travels* (1726), the greatest prose satire of modern times. His romantic attachment to Esther Johnson is revealed in his *Journal to Stella*, and in his incomparable *Correspondence*. He

is buried beside her in St Patrick's Cathedral.   Towards
the end of his life his mind gave way.

THOMSON, Sir William, Lord KELVIN (1824–1907),
physicist and inventor, was born at Belfast.   His father

Lord Kelvin

James Thomson, professor of mathematics in the Royal
Academical Institution, having been appointed to the
Chair in Glasgow University (1832), his son William
matriculated there in his eleventh year, never having
been at school.   After six years of study he left Glasgow

for Cambridge, entering Peterhouse. Here he was Senior Wrangler and first Smith's Prizeman in 1845. After taking his degree he worked for some months in Regnault's laboratory in Paris. In 1846 he was appointed professor of natural philosophy in Glasgow University, retaining the post until 1899, when he retired. For eight years (1857–66) he was engaged in the laying of the Atlantic cable, receiving a knighthood on its completion. He was created a peer in 1892. One of the greatest scientists of modern times, his work extends over almost every branch of mathematical and experimental physics, particularly thermo-dynamics, electricity, and magnetism. His life's aim was the application of science to practical ends, and this he achieved in many epoch-making discoveries and inventions. A skilled navigator, we owe to him an improved form of the mariner's compass and the sounding machine. He received the highest honours and distinctions, being a privy councillor, an honorary member of almost every foreign academy, and a doctor of almost every university. He is buried in Westminster Abbey. His numerous scientific memoirs were collected as *Electrostatics and Magnetism* (1884), *Mathematical and Physical Papers*, 6 vols. (1882–1911), *Popular Lectures and Addresses*, 3 vols. (1889–1894).

TONE, Theobald Wolfe (1763–98), United Irishman, was born in Dublin, and educated at Trinity College, where he was auditor of the Historical Society. In 1791 he succeeded Richard Burke as secretary to the Catholic Committee, and at the same time founded the society of United Irishman, with the object of reforming parliament, and removing the civil and religious grievances of the Roman Catholics. Being involved in the revolutionary designs of 1794, he fled to America with his wife and child. In the following year he was in Paris where he entered into negotiations with the Directory, including Napoleon, whom he persuaded to send an expedition to Ireland for the purpose of establishing an independent republic. The first expedition, under Hoche in 1796, was dispersed by foul weather and had to return. The second, under Bompart, Hoche being dead, sailed from Brest in September 1798, Tone, a " chef-de-brigade," being on board the *Hoche*. After a stiff fight the vessel was captured off Lough Swilly by Sir John Warren. Tone was recognised, taken to Dublin, tried, and sentenced to be hanged. His request to be shot as a French officer having been rejected, he died of a self-inflicted wound on the morning appointed for his execution. He was a man of great determination and of remarkable intellectual powers. His *Autobiography* is an historical document of great value.

TYNDALL, John (1820–93), natural philosopher, was born at Leighlin Bridge, Co. Carlow, and was for some years employed on the Ordnance Survey, subsequently spending three years as a railway engineer in England. In 1847 he was appointed teacher of mathematics at Queenwood College, Hampshire. The years 1848–51 were spent at the universities of Marburg and Berlin, where he established his reputation by investigations on the magneto-optic properties of crystals, first published in conjunction with Knoblauch (1850), and considerably extended as *Diamagnetism* (1870). In 1853 he was appointed professor of natural philosophy at the Royal Institution, where he succeeded Faraday as superintendent in 1867, a post he retained until 1887. He also succeeded him as scientific adviser to Trinity

House (1866–83). Tyndall's principal work was connected with the properties of radiant heat in its relation to gases ; on floating matter in the air in relation to putrefaction and infection, where he showed that " optically pure " air is incapable of developing bacteria. The publications by which he is best known are *The Glaciers of the Alps* (1860) in conjunction with Huxley ; *Heat as a mode of Motion* (1863), said to be his best work ; *On Sound* (1867) ; *The Forms of Water* (1872) ; and *Lectures on Light* (1873). His charm of style and wonderful gift of clear exposition made him unrivalled as a lecturer. His presidential address at the British Association in 1874 on the relations between science and theology created a profound sensation.

USSHER, James (1581–1656), Archbishop of Armagh, born in Dublin, was one of the first students admitted to Trinity College when it was opened in 1593. He was professor of divinity from 1607 to 1621, when he was appointed Bishop of Meath by James I., whose favour he had obtained during his frequent visits to England in quest of books and manuscripts. In 1624 he was consecrated Archbishop of Armagh. On the outbreak of the Rebellion in 1641 he withdrew to England, and he continued to reside there until his death. The patronage of James was continued by Charles I., whose execution Ussher actually witnessed, fainting at the sight. From 1647–55, he was lecturer at Lincoln's Inn. He died at Reigate. So great was the veneration in which he was held, that though a Royalist, Cromwell accorded him a public funeral in Westminster Abbey. Of a somewhat Calvinistic turn of mind he was constantly involved in bitter polemics. His attitude towards Catholics was one of extreme intolerance. His principal works are *Britannicarum Ecclesiarum Anti-quitates* (1639), a work of immense learning which procured him a gold medal and a letter of congratulation from Cardinal Richelieu ; *Annales Veteris et Novi Testa-*

James Ussher, Archbishop of Armagh

menti (1650–54), the first attempt to fix the chronology of the Bible, and that given in the authorised version. His voluminous writings, Latin and English, were collected in seventeen volumes by C. R. Elrington, 1847–64. The bulk of his fine library of 10,000 printed volumes and manuscripts passed to Trinity College.

WALLACE, William Vincent (1814–65), composer, born
at Waterford, was the son of a Scotch bandmaster who
subsequently removed to Dublin, and got an engagement
in the band of the Theatre Royal, where young William
played the violin. At seventeen he was appointed
organist of Thurles Cathedral. Having married, he
emigrated to New South Wales in 1835, and settled in
the bush, laying music aside. Some friends hearing
him play the violin on one of his visits to Sydney, prevailed upon him to give a concert. Afterwards he
travelled over the world giving concerts and meeting
with many strange adventures, visiting in turn Tasmania,
New Zealand, India, South and Central America, and
the United States. In 1845 he was in London, and
two years later produced at Drury Lane *Maritana*, the
opera by which he is best known. This was followed
in 1847 by *Matilda of Hungary*. After another tour
in South America (1849), he went to Germany, where he
lived for fourteen years. It was during this period that
most of his piano music was written. His *Lurline*,
produced at Covent Garden in 1860, proved even more
successful than *Maritana*. Other operas of his are *The
Amber Witch* (1861) and *Love's Triumph* (1862). He
died at the Château de Bagen in the Pyrenees, whither
he had been ordered for his health, and was buried at
Kensal Green, London.

WELLINGTON, Sir Arthur Wellesley, first Duke of
(1769–1852), was born in Dublin, at 24 Upper
Merrion Street. His father, Garrett Wellesley, Earl of
Mornington (1735–81), was the well-known musical
composer, whose beautiful glees " Here in cool grot,"
and " Come, fairest nymph," are still favourites. He
was educated at Eton and the French Military College,

Angers, where he studied under the great engineer,
Pignerol. He entered the army in 1787. From 1790–
1795 he sat in the Irish parliament for Trim, serving on
committees with Lord Edward FitzGerald. He first
saw active service in Flanders (1794). From 1797–1805
he served in India, where he distinguished himself in
the Mysore and Mahratta campaigns, winning the
decisive battle of Assaye (1803). He took part in the
bombardment of Copenhagen in 1807, and in the same
year became Chief Secretary for Ireland. In 1808 he
began his great career in the Peninsula, shattering the
power of Napoleon in a series of brilliant victories at
Talavera, Torres Vedras, Albuera, Ciudad Rodrigo,
Badajos, Salamanca, and Vitoria (1813), and entering
Paris in May 1814. For his great services he was
created a duke. On Napoleon's escape from Elba
(1815), he was in Brussels, commanding English and
Belgian armies. On June 16 he defeated Ney at
Quatre Bras, and two days later, in conjunction with
the Prussians under Blücher, finally overthrew Napoleon
in the great battle of Waterloo. His life was henceforth
devoted to diplomacy and politics. He was Prime
Minister 1820–30 and in 1834, in the conservative
interest. He is buried close to Nelson in St Paul's
Cathedral.

INDEX

T

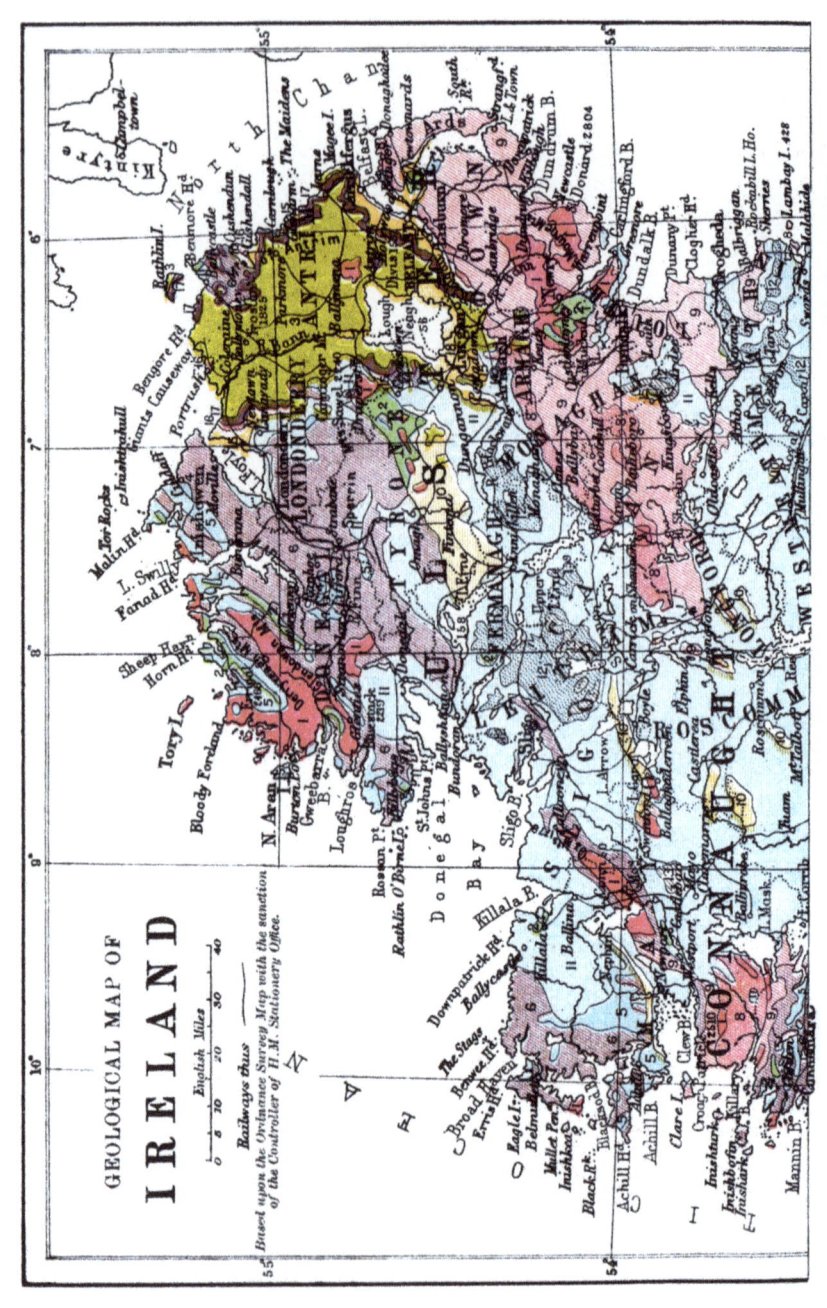

GEOLOGICAL MAP OF

IRELAND

English Miles

Railways thus

Based upon the Ordnance Survey Map with the sanction
of the Controller of H.M. Stationery Office.

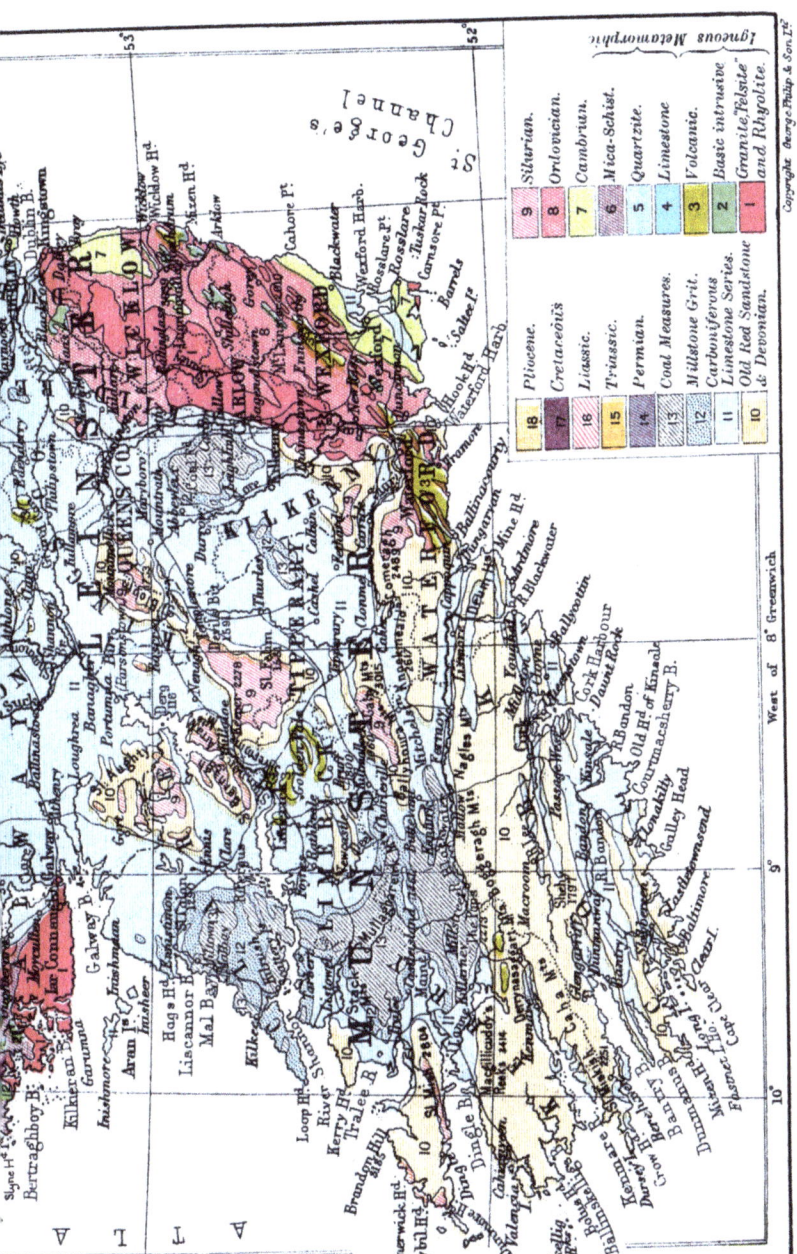

For EU product safety concerns, contact us at Calle de José Abascal, 56–1°,
28003 Madrid, Spain or eugpsr@cambridge.org.

www.ingramcontent.com/pod-product-compliance
Ingram Content Group UK Ltd.
Pitfield, Milton Keynes, MK11 3LW, UK
UKHW020507240426
470322UK00012B/253